WHERE DIVISION ENDS

"It is not impossible that it should fall to the lot of this work,
in its poverty and in the darkness of this time, to bring light
into one brain or another—but of course it is not likely."
—Wittgenstein, Preface to *Philosophical Investigations*, 1945.

Maurice Ash was born in 1917 in Bihar, India, and hence was a child of
the now all but forgotten British Empire. He finished at his public
school (Greshams, once deemed 'progressive') academically at the lowest
level possible. He took a degree in Economics at the London School of
Economics. In World War II he saw active service in the Armoured Forces
at Alamein, Italy and Greece. After the war he went to Dartington, Devon,
where he married Ruth, daughter of the founders of the Dartington Hall
Trust—a projected reincarnation of the idea of a landed estate as a complex of activities, largely modelled on Tagore's ashram in Bengal, but with
an American flavour.

Maurice and Ruth went to live and farm in Essex and had three
daughters and a son (prematurely deceased). It was during this time (the
1950s) that Maurice first encountered Wittgenstein, which radically
affected his attitude to the social sciences. After returning to Devon he
became Chairman of the Town and Country Planning Association, and
later succeeded Leonard Elmhirst as Chairman of the Dartington Hall
Trust. On his own property he established the Sharpham Trust, which
included a College of Buddhist Studies and Contemporary Enquiry. He
became the first Chairman of the Green Alliance and a member of the
Henry Moore Foundation. He has written some half-dozen books, of
which this is the last.

WHERE DIVISION ENDS

On Feeling at Home in Chaos

Maurice Ash

Green Books

First published in 2001
by Green Books Ltd
Foxhole, Dartington
Totnes, Devon TQ9 6EB

© Maurice Ash 2001

Cover design by Rick Lawrence

Text printed by Biddles Ltd, Guildford, Surrey
on Five Seasons 100% recycled paper

British Library Cataloguing in Publication Data
available on request

ISBN 1 903998 06 9

Contents

Acknowledgements

My thanks to Mary Bride Nicholson for her kindness in having typed and re-typed these pages to make the words themselves intelligible, out of her many years' familiarity with their meanings—though such labour has not at times been without inconvenience, and even hardship, to herself.

And my thanks equally to John Lane for the salutary cruelty, even at the risk of our friendship, in pointing out where the meanings of the words were, or might be, unintelligible to others.

Such kindness and such cruelty have been equally necessary to the making of this book.

A Note on the Origin of these Essays

Most of these articles have been adapted from work originally published in Resurgence magazine: *Atonement*, March 2000; *Our Tragic Metaphysics*, July 1994; *Greening of the Government*, January 1989; *The Fall and Rise of Green Politics*, January 1993; *The Hidden Agenda*, March 1989; *Town and Country (from a Buddhist Perspective)*, November 1979; *Elmhirst and Rural Life*, May 1983 (this was a reprint of a talk given at Santiniketan, Bengal, to celebrate the 60th anniversary of Elmhirst's work on rural reconstruction with Rabindranath Tagore); *False Economy*, March 1988; *Grown-up Politics*, September 1989; *Energy and Form*, May 1980; *The Great Questioning*, November 1999; *. . . or a Private Language*, March 1999; *There Is No Alternative*, November 1988; *The Tragic Century*, November 1994; *On Being and Becoming*, May 1993; *A Heroic Voice*, September 1992; *Spirit and Causation*, May 1989; *A Western Falun Gong?*, January 2001.

Foreword

In the beginning was the deed, not the word, says Maurice Ash; learning by doing is his dictum. For him, there is beauty and spirituality in everyday living. He derives his inspiration from the Buddha, from Ludwig Wittgenstein and from E. F. Schumacher.

In the West, people talk about 'theory and practice'. In this juxtaposition, theory is primary and practice is secondary: it is assumed that theory leads practice. But in the Buddhist tradition, it is the other way around. The Buddhist phrase is *achar* and *vichar*—practice then theory. For the Buddhists, practice is primary and theory secondary. Out of practising, experiencing and acting, theories may grow.

Maurice prefers deeds over words, because knowledge is implicit in action. Living emerges out of the whole being. There is a sense of wholeness in practice. Mind divides, body unites. Knowledge separates, action connects. Words touch the partial; silence touches the whole.

In this book of essays, written over a number of years, he unpicks the fallacy of fragmented and compartmentalized knowledge. Although each essay stands alone, there is an underlying theme running throughout. In every one of them you will find that he unequivocally exposes the inherent falsehood of Cartesian dualism. Whichever page you turn to, you will encounter an uncompromising critique of the dualistic paradigm.

From Maurice's perspective, the split between Self and the World, between subject and object, the observer and the observed, is at the root of the multiple crises facing Western societies. He does not waste any time or words in discussing the symptoms of our sickness; he looks at the deep causes.

He hits two targets with his powerful arrows of Buddhist logic. First, there is no substantial Self; there is no Self separate from the World. It is the current illusion of the Self which has given birth to self-centred, self-seeking, selfish and egotistical individualism. Only by moving away from the illusion of Self can we embrace the reality of community. "The world is constituted of the relationships of relationships," says the author. In Buddhist terminology it is called 'co-dependent arising'; self is a web of relationships. No independent Self, but a co-dependent self. In other words, "Only connect."

The second target Maurice Ash aims to demolish is the notion of metaphysics. It is metaphysics which gives birth to idealism, utopianism, communism, and all the other isms. For Maurice, reality is in the here and the now—it is in the way we live our everyday life.

Western societies have built huge structures of politics, economics, education, and much else, on the foundation of the individualized Self and dematerialized metaphysics. Self, having a metaphysical ideal, craves for power and control. Then it builds larger and larger structures to exercise that power and control. This turns into an addiction to power. All addictions lead to suffering. In the author's view, the way out of this suffering is to experience the world and sense every situation as a whole. Only within such wholes can we nurture a sense of place and a sense of community. Community, by nature, has to be of a human scale. In other words, small is beautiful.

These are some of the challenging ideas explored in the essays contained in this book. It is a seminal collection of ideas. It is radical thinking in robust prose. I would put this book on a par with *Small is Beautiful*. If you want to find the relevance of Buddhism to our time, then this is the book for you.

Satish Kumar
Hartland, 1st July 2001

Introduction

I HAVE decided to make no excuses for the obscurities this book may hold for any readers it may be lucky enough to attract. It could, no doubt, be converted into something of a primer for all those for whom its allusions are obscure, and no doubt its very prose could be made more felicitous. (I have not been without well-meant recommendations to this effect.) But what would be foregone by such revisions—arguably, indeed, improvements—is the sense of struggle in which the book is conceived. Its readers might well like to read what they are used to reading, expressed in the terms to which they are used, but this would be to camouflage the struggle. And it is the struggle that the book is about.

The struggle in question is to make oneself understood in a language that has declined the props of dualistic thought. This implies a rejection of the duality of the Self and the World. Since this duality lies at the root of what we suppose to be knowledge, and hence of the world we have fabricated for ourselves to live in, to challenge it is to tilt at the spell under which we have lived at least since Plato and Aristotle, but with particular intensity since the Renaissance and Descartes.

Of course, this book is only a very minor player in a transformation of our way of making sense of our lives, a way that now seems to be set and spreading. Its most obvious manifestation, perhaps, is in our environmental concerns, as also in our reactions to the exploration of space and humankind's insignificance therein; but simultaneously it is to be discerned in our changing ideas. Characteristic in this respect is the development of quantum mechanics, with its interdependence of observer and observed. Virtually simultaneously with this revolution in classical science, philosophy had begun its own transformation—and perhaps its ultimate extinction. Pre-eminent in this process was Wittgenstein. Significantly for him, it was a mid-life experience; for in his youthful *Tractatus* he had logically reduced the Self—upon which our concept of knowledge classically hinged—to a dimensionless point and had ended by advising any readers he might have had to ignore all he had written. The turn he then took was away from philosophy's immemorial love of truth and towards the question of meaning. This required abandonment of the rock of metaphysical certainty on which the old search for truth had been founded—the notion that the world must be such (and pictured as such) that language can talk about it—together with the substantiality, the apartness, of the Self that searches. We must, in brief, seek other ways 'to find our ways about'. It was a change from the absolute to the contingent.

I make no apologies, now or later, for putting little expressions such as the above by Wittgenstein in quotes but without other references to them. So far as I am concerned they are now, so to speak, in the public domain and, as I hope is by now evident, he is the pathfinder to a different way of comprehending the world—and by 'the world' I mean, now and henceforth, 'all that is the case'. I can only hope this does not prove irritating to those (are there still such?) who are quite unfamiliar with these references, or to whom their relevance is not obvious.

I should, however, perhaps say something more about an expression that appears quite frequently in my text: the substantial Self. It is anyway a puzzle, what the Self is. Cartesian doubt is centred on this question. Descartes doubted his own existence, but resolved the problem by the consolation that he thought: he had a separate existence from the solid world about which he could think. Personally, however, I think the question has a deeper stratum. God, the Creator of all that is, is the prerequisite of a substantial Self. Moreover, this God must be the sole God (perhaps the ultimate metaphysic) otherwise the substantiality of the Self would not be verifiable by beings in thrall to other gods. (Hence the poignancy in our war cemeteries of the inscription above every unknown soldier's grave of Kipling's words: "Known only to God".) In other words, monotheism and the substantiality of the Self—and therewith the subject-object basis of our idea of knowledge and truth—are interdependent.

This last point might seem abstruse to the point of irrelevance were it not for one fact: many of the essays in this book touch on Buddhism, and Buddhism, though it is much concerned with the Self, is a non-theistic faith. Hence, for Buddhism, the Self is insubstantial. I do not think it is necessary to go further into this point here, except perhaps to suggest it might be pertinent to finding our way about in a world lost to metaphysical certainties.

This does, however, lead to a truly significant point: namely, the quite extraordinary affinities that have been found in the last twenty-five years between Wittgenstein's thought and that of the generally acknowledged greatest of Buddhist thinkers, Nagarjuna, who lived in about AD 200, some 500 years after Buddha himself, who had lived in an era of oral communication. I myself was led to an interest in Buddhism through my awareness of Wittgenstein. (I do not call myself a 'Buddhist'.) This interest did not stem from any study of the Buddhist texts, but rather from the similarity of their ideas of reality, though Wittgenstein knew little or nothing of Buddhism. This, in turn, has belatedly led me to think—indeed, to feel an obligation—that I should seek a compatibility between the consuming interests of my adult span of life.

But should this sort of compatibility concern any of us? I have always surreptitiously envied whoever it was who said: "I contradict myself: very well, I contradict myself"—yet I could not actually condone such irresponsibility. However, when one is old, say, should one be held to account for the opinions of one's youth? And in one set of circumstances must the values of another set hold constant? Put another way, is there really no such thing as society?—for how could people be socially bound together if there were no consistency in their values? Would it be tenable for each and all of us to hold opinions in one range of activities that were somehow incompatible with our opinions in some other range? And how could we live with ourselves if we did so? Well, I suspect such aberrations are indeed the case, but I also do not doubt there is such a thing as society. At all events, a prime motive in my putting these essays in the covers of one book was to discover whether philosophically they held reasonably well together; for, in truth, I had never stopped to wonder whether my interests in social studies, in economics, in education, in agriculture or land-use planning were compatible with my religious interests and, in particular, in Buddhism. Hence, this has been a quasi-autobiographical exercise—but not, I hope, in the current fashion of that mode: as a pursuit (and justification) of the Self.

In this exercise, Buddhism itself has been instructive. For Buddhism has always adapted itself to whichever societies it has spread. It carries no prescriptions for how society itself should be conducted. Indeed, in the Tibetan language there is not even a word for 'society', and in Sanskrit, I understand, one would be hard put to find one. That the householder should be responsible for the curtilage of his dwelling seems to be about as far as Buddhism penetrates the society of most Buddhist countries. And yet, that these countries are Buddhist seems self-evident. Buddhism merely helps those who live in them to 'find their way about'.

It is inconceivable, for instance, that Buddhism should proselytize for democracy—at least, as the West understands this. Should it do so, it would quickly be faced with the observations of de Tocqueville, the greatest historian of democracy, about the essential sameness of democrats, born and bred, and the consequent loss of richness in their culture;

indeed, as de Tocqueville persuasively showed, egalitarian egoism is at the root of centralized power. People who have succumbed to technological causation live in Eliot's *Waste Land*,
in which there is only a past and a future. "Technology and
everything that goes with it", says H. L. Finch, "has no present. And people who live in that world live in a ghost world
without a present." They come alive only when hopelessly
stuck in a traffic jam—and switch the engine off. Ah, what
peace! It is likewise, and for obvious reasons, unlikely that
Buddhism would proselytize for even an enlightened autoc-
racy. (Plato's philosopher king perhaps remains the most
destructive of Western prescriptions.) The emperor Asoka
would be a token, durable over the centuries, of the folly of
literally staking out, post by post, even so vast an empire as
India to rest under Buddhist rule. Nevertheless, the infiltration
of Buddhism into any society might go a long way towards
neutralizing the immemorial plague of the Western world:
namely, the inherently false reality of idealism, together with
its degeneration into ideology. At most, perhaps, Buddhism
might be expected to influence the localization of life and
significantly to mitigate the giantism of scale to which the
pervasive technologies of our corrupt form of knowledge is
so conducive. But all this, and much else, is the staple of further discussion.

To conclude this Introduction on a personal note, what
follow are essays culled from the magazine *Resurgence* over the
past quarter-century, but now modified in greater or lesser
degree for present publication. They are not arranged chrono-
logically, but rather thematically—and loosely, at that, and
without much linear continuity; they may, therefore, make
undue demands on readers' memories of the historical
moments that gave rise to some of them. I can only apologize
for this. But more to the point is why they were ever published at all, for I received scarcely any reactions, oral or written, to any of them from readers of the magazine. When I
confronted the Editor, Satish Kumar, about this, I gathered he

had sensed an attempt on my part to struggle free from the conventions of Western, mechanistic thought—and that, I suppose, is indeed what it amounted to. For this I would surely have to thank the upbringing of Satish in the Jain tradition. In any event, I think that by now the state of disillusion with how we have chosen to manage the affairs of our world—a disillusionment of which the arts are perhaps a prime, if inadvertent, manifestation—has reached a pitch where the record of one person's struggle, no matter how feeble, to confront that disillusion, might begin to be of interest.

Chapter One

Beginnings

Atonement

THE SUBJECT of an object and the object of a subject are both metaphysical tools, even if they do constitute the classical means of the Western, or dualistic, search for knowledge—whether this be by rational means, or empirically through the senses. Both subject and object are unreal abstractions, and any knowledge they disclose (and it has been astounding) must be strongly qualified. It is now time to start considering how our lives might be different if we obeyed another, holistic, epistemology.

It would seem natural enough to begin with the question of education. As we understand it today, education is a practice engaged in between teachers and taught and is concerned with the transmission of knowledge. In this process the teacher as subject—one who holds the key to understanding—conveys knowledge to the pupil as object—one who must be endowed with understanding. But what, in this singular process, is taught by the teacher is, or has been, itself an object. Hence object is taught to object and no knowledge is generated. Dualistic teaching is theoretically sterile. Teaching (and testing) by rote is the most extreme example of this proposition; it is a recipe for ignorance and sterility. Should anything be learnt in such a classroom (as maybe it none the less will be), it will most probably be through some variable of what is already known, possibly through a teacher's unconventionality, or by what the pupils teach one another. In the process, however, 'knowledge' must (perhaps imperceptibly) change.

All this (or something like it) is conventional wisdom. For the sake of completeness, however, it would be as well to ask, why should not an object (a pupil) become itself a subject? After all, we are not dealing here in essences: only in metaphysics.

The answer must be, I think, because of the psychology of such a shift; there is a psychology in changing, say, from pupil to teacher, not least to self-teacher. One can, of course, 'discover', rather than 'learn', knowledge by oneself. Yet in so far as we are here puzzling about metaphysical, and hence insubstantial, concepts, there may nevertheless be a psychology involved in exchanging one illusion for another. This shadow rests over the whole notion of the knowledge by which we commonly abide.

Dualistic knowledge, in brief, is inherently flawed. The flaw lies in the actual interdependence of everything, and is disclosed by the artificial separation of subject and object. (Put differently, the actual world is not a laboratory.) Yet upon this flaw vast areas of human life have been structured through its inherent premise of causation—which follows from the isolation of object and subject in time and space—and all the consequent, anguish of a First Cause, etc.

So if it is from our conventional idea of education that such doubts as these arise, are they not enough to throw the very concept into question? Perhaps they are—but it would be salutary to recall the foresight of Adam Smith about education. He recognized that an inexorable con?equence of the operation of his Hidden Hand in the market would be the ever greater disadvantage of the uneducated to the benefit of the educated. He therefore advocated universal education as the concomitant of Free Trade. Admirable liberal sentiments! — and over the next 200 years they have put 'Education, Education, Education' at the centre of politics, but at the cost of the tail wagging the dog. As the scale of industry and economic structures generally has increased, so has that of schools.

Education has lost its human scale. And what if, as seems likely, the idea of knowledge on which it is based is flawed, and very possibly lies at the root of the environmental anxieties so closely related to the Hidden Hand? Should not a different source of education be sought? Let the question stand.

THIS LEADS readily enough to another metaphysical form of life: the economy. The economy has come to be thought of as the equivalent of a natural phenomenon, and measurable as such. Yet it is but a reification, a contrived thing, as much a machine as the human body, the verisimilitude of which derives from a reduction of the intentions of human actions to a common denominator of utility. For utility can be made measurable by the price mechanism, such that only what is measurable is really real!

Yet, of course, human beings are motivated by a whole complex of passions—not least the ambition of economists themselves to be deemed as scientific as physicists—whilst in fact the descriptions of what is to be measured in economics, the statistical entities, are scientifically speaking arbitrary, to the point of being a standing joke (cf. GDP and road accidents). And as E. F. Schumacher pointed out in his potent chapter on Buddhist Economics, the cost of labour premised as a factor of production in classical economics is in some 'economies' its precise opposite.*

At all events, economists have contrived the economy as an object for their subjective analysis—an analysis dependent on the metaphysical properties of money as the proxy of value. It is scarcely surprising, then, that those who think of themselves as the masters of the world economy—the Central Bankers and the Finance Ministers—themselves do not understand the 'irrational behaviour' of the money markets, and really do not know what to do about it.

---

* See *Small is Beautiful*.

NEXT, consider the environment. The environment has recently become a thing, like any other. It is now thought of as an object, subject to management by human beings having a dualistic understanding of it, as of object and subject. But how can a thing itself have no environment? And if the environment is a thing, what is its own environment? Obviously, only metaphysics could resolve this little miracle. Or alternatively it has to be accepted that the environment is susceptible only to holistic, not to dualistic, understanding: which is as much as to allow our feelings to have a say in the issue. If the consequences of this misunderstanding—perhaps ultimate misunderstanding—of the nature of knowledge were not potentially so dire, this misuse of it would be almost comic.

NEXT, what might be said of cities and their planning? We still hold to the belief that our cities might be planned: patently, their state is often desperate enough to justify this assumption. The 'thingness' of a city, what fixes it as an object apart, stems, surely, from the walls whereby cities were historically determined.

This idea—or, rather, illusion—of self-containment of cities persists to this day, at least in Britain, in the shape of the Green Belt. (In Paris the walls themselves lasted almost into living memory—but the French have long since rejected the concept of the Green Belt.) Much of the urban disaster we still call 'London' can be ascribed to the presumption that it is contained within its Green Belt.

Yet, just as "no man is an island, unto himself entire," nor is, nor ever was, any city. This is dimly appreciated today by those urban planners who practise regionally—and planners, after all, are the only social practitioners whose calling obliges them to think holistically. But their political masters remain enthralled, against all common sense, by a regressive metaphysical picture of the city. To renounce this picture, after all, would be to renounce their power.

Sadly, when cities were cities, their citizens were part of

them and they of their citizens. Today, when we analyse and plan them, nobody belongs to anything—or only weakly so.

WHAT OF agriculture? On the face of it, what could be more real, less metaphysical, than farming? But farming today is not what farming was. The very word has bewitched us.

Historically, one only has to hark back to the medieval open-field system to begin to realize this. That land was farmed by farmers, but in a way we today would find unrecognizable. The community took all the decisions about what, where and by whom the land would be farmed. Technologically—to our eyes, though not by what had preceded it—such farming was virtually primitive. But it was not done for a market—rather for barter, or self-consumption, or the Church. Farming was not, therefore, an abstract activity. Monetary values scarcely determined it. The values of farming were then inextricably entangled with those of the community.

Today, conversely, they are discretely defined by monetary units. And in pursuit of those units outrage is now done, whether to the soil, to the animals, or to those whom 'farming' feeds.

So farming today, like so much else, has become a discrete activity: one for which the explanation is to be sought in its market situation. And the explanation of its market—not how it is, but that it is? Not, to be sure, in the Church and its saints, or residual pagan gods, as would have been the case with the old open-field system, but rather, if anything, in the metaphysics of nihilism. That is, if a thing can be done with genes, or hormones, or waste—it should be done. Such things are self-justifying.

Such farming, however, need not be accepted. The soil can be reconstituted and its products restored. To do this might imply a restructured rural life, one with shorter 'food miles', for instance, and, above all, a different method of accounting. For are discrete monetary units the only expressions of value given to us? What an impoverishment of life that would be, if it were so!

Rather, values can be expressed by, say, dancing, or perhaps by carnival to celebrate the achievements—or the disasters—of a harvest. These are not fey or frivolous suggestions; they simply foreshadow a society more co-operative than our present mindset can seriously entertain. But not beyond a mindset that the environmental exigencies of the next hundred years might again bring us to adopt.

ONE COULD go on, indefinitely. The seeds have been sown for huge changes in the Western world over the next (say) hundred years; it needs only the collapse of our fantasy of an economy to let them sprout. It is worth remembering that in his post-War despondency Wittgenstein wrote: "It is not impossible that it should fall to the lot of this work, in its poverty and in the darkness of this time, to bring light into one brain or another—but of course it is not likely." Though what he wrote challenged the very roots of Western thought, it has, astonishingly, spread. Yet he himself had only vague intimations of the possibilities for great changes carried by his thought—and perhaps, anyway, it is not so much thoughts as events that are themselves the agents of change.

In any case it is notable that though Western art has borrowed much from other cultures over the last century, and not least from the most primitive ones, we have learnt nothing from the forms of those societies themselves. Meanwhile Western art itself, reduced as it is to mere sensation, serves little more than to cover the vacancy of our lives. But the potlatch of the North American Indians, for instance, surely has much to say to the gross wealth and the growing inequalities of the late twentieth century. And the same is true of any culture stemming from an holistic epistemology.

This speck of a world, spinning precariously in the void, carries indifferently an invisible burden of human shame at our maltreatment of it. What we have done is, alas, irreversible. But, if only for our own preservation, we should be ready to make a new start should, through some catastrophe, the opportunity occur, and not seek to re-make things in the old way. Such an atonement is the least we owe for the miracle of our sojourn here.

Meanwhile, I suppose, like the Falun Gong in China, it's each to his own monastery. For if it is the case—as indeed it is—that 'the meaning of a word is its use in the language', then we who use words must perforce be humble. We cannot truly know to what they refer—nor Truth itself. But we can still use language homoeopathically: in small doses, to cure the sickness it has created.

A Prophet of our Times

THE WAY Wittgenstein lived his life matters for an understanding of what he wrote and, as such, it matters more than our own lives usually matter; for we can read in his life what he wrote in his book, which itself is indeed hard to understand, whereas most people's books are, albeit inadvertently, a cover for their lives. What he wrote, actually, was but a prolonged conversation with himself. He did not presume, as most of us tend to do, that his life was just another thing detached from himself. ("Genius", H. L. Finch suggests, in writing of Wittgenstein, "is the ability to live without an identity.")

Wittgenstein's language was virtually synonymous with his living. Consider, for example: " 'But you will surely admit that there is a difference between pain-behaviour accompanied by pain and pain-behaviour without any pain?'—Admit it? What greater difference could there be? 'And yet you again and again reach the conclusion that the sensation is nothing.' Not at all. It is not a something, but not a nothing either. The conclusion was only that a nothing would serve just as well as a something about which nothing could be said. We have only rejected the grammar that tries to force itself upon us here."

It was considerations such as these which led Finch, in his study of Wittgenstein, to say: "So far as I knew, this is the first time in Western thought when the starting point for thought was not, in however disguised a way, a subject and object, which a philosopher then attempted to relate to each other." So this is why a very good introduction to the philosopher we call Wittgenstein is not through his writings themselves but, rather, through a book such as *Wittgenstein's Vienna*, by Allan Janik and Stephen Toulmin.

Wittgenstein's Vienna was indeed the precursor of our own anguished times. It was all too like 'cool Britain', the capital of kitsch, in which the inept centralist and secretive Hapsburg regime kept at bay any serious involvement of its people with the evolution of its affairs. In our own 'elective dictatorship', with its pervasive tabloid culture, are not ever fewer people interested in, and more cynical of, politics? Vienna had some of the most shameful housing conditions in Europe, widespread prostitution, perennial scandals and suicides and local racial unrest, together with all the debilitations of the great 1872 Stock Exchange crash—the big one before its successor in 1929 (and before the next one in another seventy years, as one theory has it?). Vienna was, in the mordant expression of one of its participants, a proving ground for humankind's destruction and, sure enough, the Great War blew it all away.

Not surprisingly, this climate became a pressure cooker of those determined to distinguish appearances from reality: Schoenberg and Mahler in music, Klimt and Kokoschka in painting, Loos in architecture (the predecessor of the Bauhaus, which, some say, debased his vision), Boltzman in thermodynamics, Rilke in poetry, Freud with psychoanalysis. Vienna also bred Hitler and his social impulses from the purity of *Nature*—and Wittgenstein was his contemporary at the Linza Realschule—just as (with what irony!) it nurtured Hertzl, the founder of Zionism. Wittgenstein's father was of part Jewish and assimilated Christianized stock; he became the immensely rich steelmaster of the Austro-Hungarian Empire, and his house a cultural meeting place of Vienna. (After the War, Wittgenstein gave away the immense fortune he inherited, which had been protected by investment in America.) Kierkegaard and Tolstoy were primary intellectual influences in this seething, decadent melting-pot of a Vienna, to all of which the maturation of Wittgenstein was contingent.

Of course, *Wittgenstein's Vienna* is not without serious discussion of the development of Wittgenstein's thought itself. Far from it, but much of this development took place in very different surroundings, not least in the utter solitude of the hut he built himself in a remote Norwegian fjord, and as a front-line (and much decorated) soldier of the Austro-Hungarian army in the Great War.

It is hard not to conclude, however, that the prime influence on his first book, the *Tractatus*, was his contact at Cambridge with the world of academic philosophy, the world of Bertrand Russell and G. E. Moore. For it is such a philosophical book! That is to say, it all but destroyed the ruling solipsism of Cartesian thought—'the world is my world'—by reducing the Self of Descartes to a non-dimensional point; and concluding (almost): "My propositions serve as elucidations in the following way: anyone who understands me eventually recognizes them as nonsensical. . . . He must transcend these propositions, and then he will see the world aright."

It was in the same mood that later, in vainly seeking a publisher, he wrote that he offered two books, the one he had written and the one he had not written and it was the latter book that contained all that mattered. His life was that other book. And, of course, he actually concluded the *Tractatus* with: "Whereof one cannot speak one must be silent." As for Bertrand Russell, he ceased doing philosophy—except for potboilers—once Wittgenstein, as a student, had pointed out the fatal flaw in his magnum opus, the *Principia Mathematica*. The perpetual adulation of Russell by the British media as the philosophical genius of the century could stand as good a

symbol as any of Britain's intellectual insulation from the
world at large. Perhaps the BBC's choice of Russell after the
war to be the first (hugely successful) Reith Lecturer says as
much about Britain as the loss of its Empire.

And so for a decade Wittgenstein let things be, quite fal-
low of philosophy. When he returned to it it was to a whole
world showing symptoms of the sickness of Vienna—with
one significant addition. Philosophy, of itself, seemed to
Wittgenstein a sickness. And the sickness lay in the very
medium in which it was conducted: in language itself. Hence
the only justification for doing philosophy was to conduct the
struggle against "the bewitchment of our intelligence by language". Such a practice was a kind of therapy, a healing: and
so, presumably, to be conducted 'homoeopathically'—used in
small doses and in ordinary language.

What this did (and is doing) is to question the basic construction of the world as we have tried to make sense of it.
Our faculty of speech itself has betrayed us into an illusion of
the intelligibility of the world. Fundamentally, this means our
questioning the ideal, which "as we think of it, is unshake-
able. You can never get outside it; you must always turn back.
There is no outside; outside you cannot breathe. Where does
this idea come from? It is like a pair of glasses on our nose
through which we see whatever we look at. It never occurs
to us to take them off." Consequently, "When you are doing
philosophy you have to descend into primaeval chaos and
feel at home there." Perhaps it is no wonder people have
found him difficult!

The "chaos" in which Wittgenstein felt at home was,
presumably, a world without subject and object. Reality for
Wittgenstein is anchored in notions such as language
games, which are the interplay between language and
everyday life: forms of life, which are our manifold everyday practices, to justify which we can ultimately only say,
when reason can take us no further, "my spade is turned":
and the natural history of human beings, which is our ani-

mal existence—or, if you prefer, in W. B. Yeats' phrase, "the fury and the mire of human veins". The Platonic primacy of Reason does not figure here any more. The reality of language has annulled it.

This may seem a strange way to make sense of the world (and oneself), but it is not unique—or even, strictly, original. It was conveyed in Nagarjuna's *Verses from the Center*, by general consent the written text of the basic teachings of Buddha (translated by Stephen Batchelor in 2000, from the Tibetan), and stemming from the notion of 'co-dependent origination' and the interdependence of everything; and it was also expressed by Lao Tzu: "The Tao that can be spoken of is not the Tao that is." These beginnings of Oriental understanding sent their culture off in such divergent ways from the West that until recently they have remained all but incomprehensible to us, and until recently likewise such understanding as we had of them came from debased Hindu sources—and 'Hindu' itself was a Western fabrication, stemming from our compulsion to taxonomize. It may be, however, that quantum mechanics (and chemistry) will now bring together these two great streams of human understanding; but to develop that here would be a case of fools rushing in where angels fear to tread.

At all events, however, there is no longer any doubting the quite extraordinary affinities of Wittgenstein's approach with that of Buddhism, and Nagarjuna in particular. A pioneer of this perception was Chris Gudmunsen in his book of 1977, *Wittgenstein and Buddhism*.

Whether or not, however, some conjunction of East and West will occur, one can surely contend it was Wittgenstein who opened a chink in the walls of the prison house of Western thought—with its ideologies, its solipsisms and the sheer monotony of its mechanistic processes—a chink through which one can perceive that there lies a land beyond.

Chapter Two

Beyond the Age
of Metaphysics

Our Tragic Metaphysics

WE TAKE it for granted—the Self. We fabricate some substance for it, and it is fixed in our lives. It is so because it is crucial to our making sense of the world. Yet it is but a metaphysic that causes and has caused us incalculable hardship and travail.

The Self stands on one side of a great divide, and the world on the other. Perhaps because of the immeasurable width of this divide the Self carries connotations of the Soul: that of which the utter aloneness enhallows it. This division goes far back in the history of our culture: at least as far back as to when we were enjoined to render unto Caesar that which was Caesar's, and to God that which was God's. For if the Soul could be saved or damned, as by virtue of its inherent immortality it inescapably will be, it could only conceivably be so in the hands of God. God, then, is simply a necessary construct of the Self.

There remains, logically, the need to account for why it should be in one's own interest—that of the Self—that there should be justice in the world. Suffice to say, for the present, that the wrack of this Western puzzlement is now strewn all around us on the falling tide of our civilization—in the form of human rights, national sovereignty, liberty, equality, even animal rights, etc, etc,: all the effusions of Locke, Hobbes, Kant, Hegel, Marx and the rest.

PERHAPS the most notable characteristic of this wrack left by our way of understanding the world is the sheer scale of things. It is somewhat ironic that the subject-object mode of knowledge, which allows of the nearly infinite sub-division of the world into measurable particles, should also have allowed of the ever larger scale on which we conduct our affairs and, moreover, that this scale itself should have been subjected to so little examination. Perhaps this has been the case because there is so obviously a qualitative dimension to all our constructions and contrivances—things are of a right size, more or less—and this inhibits their precise examination? If so, it would help account for our (Western) tendency to apply technology whenever it exists to be applied. If something can be done, it will be done!

And then we wonder why we live such impoverished lives on the plane of meaning!

Of course, our culture has been curious, immemorially so, about its tool for knowledge, the Self. 'Know thyself' has been an injunction at least since Plato's time. But, alas, since there is ultimately nothing to be found but a metaphysical artifact, we are left only with our needs; and the ultimate need is need itself. We need to need. What an impoverished outcome of our search!

Yet this is not a plea that we close Pandora's Box, or disinvent the machine and somehow return to Eden. If anything, it is simply a plea (and a warning) that we do not resort to any belief to enrich our lives, and certainly not to beliefs of the New Age kind. For belief sustains the metaphysical Self. It, and all its paraphernalia, precedes experience, and is fixed; and, though anyone may adhere to any belief, in its fixity it is congenial to the metaphysical Self.

Faith, conversely, is born of experience and is forever adapting to it, yet is not cast down by it. Just as Wittgenstein once said he could not help but see everything from a religious point of view, so faith chases the Self out of our lives—and, in so doing, enables us to live with whatever comes out of Pandora's

Box. For faith is like the wind, that bloweth where it listeth. We hear it, but whence it comes and where it goes, we know not.

Alas, however, ours has been a belief-dominated civilization; a culture apparently confirmed by the assurance of one's existence because one thinks, and because God would not deceive us (said Descartes) about what might otherwise fill the gap between the Self and the world.

So the accoutrements of God have had to be contrived and assured, and on the foundation of this assurance our knowledge has been cultivated. Not only (it would seem) do we really exist because we think—cf. Descartes—but we also exist separately from the world at large. And our thinking privileges us to know of the world in its discrete parts. The world is a world of objects and is constituted as such in logical extension from the Self. And yet it is nothing but a contrivance of metaphysical language, derived from the causal influence of God.

Because that is all it is—a metaphysical contrivance—there have been no constraints on its growth. The scale of things is out of control; reality is out of our reach. The world metaphysical system—the economy, the balance of power, etc—is just so many words. We do not control it. All we control are the words.

Yet the tragedy is not only on the large scale, but even more so on the small. The individual too must be validated as a substantial reality, and hence the emphasis on a person's sexuality—an almost obsessional concern of our present times, which Freud's pseudo-science exemplifies. If people are sexually not 'normal' they may, covertly or openly, be deemed physically or morally sick, and their very lives tormented—but they all the more exist.

Perhaps fortunately (and for whatever reason) the meaning of 'normality' has nowadays become sufficiently diluted that this particular test for the Self's reality has lost some of its force—and sexual 'normality' itself has even become slightly unreal. In other times and in other cultures, after all, a certain abnormality was scarcely remarkable, and the greatest love poetry of the greatest of poets was unashamedly centred on it. There are still plenty of other such tests of reality, however—not least conformity to fashion, and all the peer pressures of adolescence—to sustain the tyrannies of metaphysics. It remains a modest amusement to witness the consternation of intellectual urban visitors to the countryside when they see cows in season bulling. Such inexplicable (and slightly absurd) behaviour cannot surely be natural! One has to explain that cows are not blessed with a metaphysical vocabulary.

The raging solipsism of our times, however, has in general to be seen as a reaction against the Humanism of the not-so-distant past, now seen as the arrogance of humankind responsible, by its abuse of the natural world, for the looming environmental catastrophe. Yet the wheel turns full circle, for Humanism itself is only intelligible as a product of the metaphysical Self: of the power of the knowledge acquired by the dualism of Self and World. It does indeed seem that unless we can get rid of this idea of a substantial Self we shall be caught in the unremitting cycle of its sorrows.

On Holism and Meaning

ONE HAS only to consider our sad, sprawling, amorphous suburbs to see a reflection of ourselves as we would want to be: separate—or as separate from the world as one's circumstances allow—from a world itself no longer of much significance, but inescapable. The pathos of this scenario is that both the busy world from which one has been extruded and the unreal world in which one finds oneself are equally the product of that Self which is the fulcrum of our values.

But it does not have to be like this. Descartes invoked his thinking to substantiate the fact of his own existence and we owe the Cartesian world that ensued to the dualistic thought—the relationship of subject and object—sanctioned thereby. But Descartes' philosophy itself has long since been discredited

(Wittgenstein assuredly only finished him off). The reality of what dualistic knowledge has produced is daily brought ever more into question as its environmental consequences—which dualism would precisely exclude—overshadow our futures.

This is why a post-Cartesian paradigm is emerging: a paradigm of thought which dispenses with the substantial Self. This is called holistic thought, and its most obvious characteristic is localism. On the mundane level, this is evidenced in the awkward concept of subsidiarity: the concession by the European Union that action should be taken at a local level provided it could be as well done there as centrally. When first proclaimed, this had the air of a grand concession—and was (and is) insulting to boot. Yet, far more profoundly, it implies the taking of different actions in pursuit of different values: those generated by local life, not by a faceless bureaucracy whose values are those consistent with abstractions from the world.

This word 'subsidiarity' has portended a revolution in our thoughts. Implicitly it allows the question of scale into our systems of values, and in so doing it not only rebuts the supremacy of economic measurement—and therewith the pretensions of economics themselves—but it admits the essential complexity of all our decisions. And, in turn, this complexity accepts the reality of the flexibility of language—such that 'poverty', say, may have a different meaning in one context than it does in another—and hence the provisionality of all measurement. This, it might seem, points to 'the environment' as the proper field of knowledge; but, if this were to treat of the environment as itself a thing, it would be disastrous. For what would then be the environment of the environment? No thing exists without being in some environment. To suppose otherwise is the way to totalitarianism. It would be better to accept, surely, that what surrounds us is not 'the environment', but a mystery. "The meaning of the world", said Wittgenstein, "must be outside the world."

Historically, Nature has played the part of environment in normal discourse, and in general these concepts are still all too transposable. For, logically, the concept of Nature is the ultimate reification of our governing thought processes: all that in the material world exists, apart from the detached, observing Self. Once that departure point for our pursuit of knowledge about the world is established, the idea of Nature necessarily follows. It, is, indeed, long and deeply engrained in Western culture. St Augustine could pronounce that what was contrary to Nature was evil: it was the palpable surrogate for God's word.

This, of course, is to leave open what is and is not 'natural'. The concept was used by the Church, for instance, to lay down that the only permissible sexual congress is for the procreation of children. Perhaps awareness of it could be traced back to the rite of circumcision: to the cutting off of the Self from the natural world. (Abraham was told by God that by this act he should discover his identity: change his name, and become the leader of a great nation.)

At all events, the concept of Nature is as unknown to Buddhist thought as the notion of Self is deemed insubstantiable by it; in the Tibetan language there is simply no word for it. In the West, however, its use is at the root of the shameful bias in 'Green' attitudes towards physical as opposed to social concerns. Over and beyond this, it (Nature) is accountable for the Western search for universal laws, a search leading to ever more arid deserts of meaninglessness.

We have thus been laid under the tutelage of a suffocating metaphysical tyranny: the tyranny of a quite illusory fiction. It is a tyranny analogous to that which by now also deeply permeates our increasingly cynical politics: a politics of grandiose principles, matching the scale on which our minds so proudly range, but serving only to disguise our unregenerate egoism, the supposedly enduring Self of each one of us.

It hardly needs stressing that virtually all the foregoing stems from the West's pursuit of a certain idea of knowledge. Because this idea entails a process of abstraction, its application is intrinsically incapable of taking account of the consequences of any such application for any thing or body

excluded from that abstraction. As a result, the West has
brought upon itself and the world at large all manner of
impending catastrophes. For sure, the validity of this form of
knowledge is now in question in its own right. Since it
derives from an unconscious belief in the existence of a substantial Self, it is worth surmising what could have implanted
so powerful an agent in the Western mentality.

And it must surely derive from God: that is, from our relationship to a personal God; in other words, from monotheism. Only such a relationship, it would seem, could
conceivably have given us such a conceit of ourselves: the
conceit that our Self is the fulcrum on which the explanation
of the universe turns. If this is true, then, it is paramount that
we should disabuse ourselves of all the presumptuous and
confused metaphysics reinforcing such a notion of the Self.
We have some hard thinking to do.

However, this is but to recognize the enormity of the task.
For the world we have contrived for ourselves—and at an
exponential rate—takes for granted the notion of causation,
which is integral to the idea of knowledge deriving from the
Self. And how does one start to deconstruct a world imbued
with so pervasive, so *a priori*, a concept? That it will somehow
have to be questioned follows, hopefully, from quantum
mechanics and the Uncertainty Principle, with all the intimacy, the non-detachment of relationships they bespeak.

For Buddhists, of course, the notion of Creation, or of a
First Cause, has always been problematic, indeed profoundly
misconceived. It is unlikely, however, that, mere intellectual
questioning, no matter how rigorous, could go far to dislodge
so deeply engrained a premise of our culture: nor, for that
matter, could we again rest on a myth—even so profound a
one as the god, Janus, the two-faced one—to embody the
mystery of causation. Perhaps, rather, the change will come
about by a questioning of a prime attribute of this key notion
of ours, the notion that any cause of change is separately identifiable, other than as a statistical phenomenon: the attribute,

namely, of the preponderant masculinity of a world ordered on that premise.

Admittedly, this is to draw a bow at a venture. But *prima facie* a consequence of our emphasis on the identification of causation is to emphasize the active, rather than the passive, principle. Mechanistic thought is characteristically masculine. It is the current challenge to this attitude—think only of the controversy over women priests in the Anglican Church—which lends hope that, in a largely instinctual way, the all-pervasive belief in the instrumentality of causation might indeed be unmanned. Perhaps we shall know this happy dawn of a different sense of reality has arrived when, for instance, all talk in our worldly affairs about 'mission statements' (how can such portentous jargon ever have obtained currency?) will, with its implicit relationship between effect and cause, have passed into oblivion.

Yet the implications of the centrality of the Self to our thought go still deeper. The Self has needs; it stands over against the world, and justifies itself to itself by what it can get out of that world. Its appetite is almost inexhaustible. 'Almost', because there comes a point when any further plundering of the world seems not so much physically impossible as pointless. Thus, when it is said that the Western world is headed for a future in which still greater numbers will be permanently unemployed, this is as much as to say there will be no more need for people's services, because our needs themselves are approaching exhaustion. And, in one sense, so they surely are! The trivialization of our needs can only go so far before the Self from which they stem loses its very self-respect. When the Self is devalued, we have the grounds of a bread and circuses society.

But needs merge into wants, particularly those concerning personal health, and a principal supplier of these—a main reinforcement of the Self's illusions—has become the State. Not surprisingly, then, its bureaucracy grows inexorably, and spreads . . . and this despite the avowal of politicians, even when in power, to cut it back. Such politicians, in particular, are those professing a belief in 'the individual', but the more individualistic we become, the more conformist we are.

The very measurement of people's needs and wants imposes uniformity upon them—and as this happens, the power of the political centre grows, for there can only be one measure of the measure itself, and politics becomes an ever more sterile, and a more emotionally deprived, activity. We shall not escape from the tentacles of this vicious circle unless and until the State itself, and all that follows from it, reverts to local control.

One speaks here of local control and local life because, whereas the contradictions between the Self and the world lead inexorably to the abstractions in terms of which that world is understood and possessed, conversely a situation in which Self and world were part of one another would be intimate and local.

Such a situation, however, would necessarily be characterized by the pursuit, not of knowledge, but of meaning. Meaning is a function of relationships, of the interdependence of things (just as all the topics being discussed here—and many others not discussed—are interdependent). Is it not indeed self-evident that in these times the emphasis of people's interest is changing from knowledge to meaning? Also there is a feeling afoot that knowledge is becoming increasingly meaningless. This is so, despite the notorious claim of some scientists that they are but a step from understanding 'the mind of God', as if that too might be meaningless. This should not be surprising, for the foundations of this local orientation of life in all its intimacy were laid by Wittgenstein's rejection of the hitherto immemorial presumption that language, with its grand abstractions—indeed, especially with its grand abstractions—depicts reality. This was a strong repudiation of any notion of a substantial Self.

This repudiation carries with it, inexorably, the rejection of a call upon any metaphysical power outside the conversation in terms of which we must conduct our lives as best we can.

This is not necessarily a rejection of religion, but only of the tyrannies of dogma. If anything, it bespeaks a religion that celebrates with appropriate ritual the playfulness of life, the theatre that it actually is. Nor would this preclude the taking of emergency powers for an enforcement of environmental rules to counteract the burgeoning crisis that the old way of life is bringing upon the world. It goes without saying, indeed, that vast changes in lifestyle will be imposed on the West by the environmental impact that the spread of its practices to the world at large will generate.

To take a leaf out of the Buddhist book, the West will have to learn the meaning of Beginner's Mind. Yet this is precisely not tantamount to the all-too-familiar call for a 'spiritual renaissance'. Spirit is not the opposite of matter, nor can spirit imbue what is not congenial to it. Rather, we are due for a painstaking questioning of our assumptions all along the fault line running through our culture—between subjective and objective, ideal and real, from Plato down through the divisions, alas, between the 'fundis' and the 'realos' of every Green Party today: even, eventually, between the distinction of noun and verb that constitutes the very grammar of our discourse, and which serves to keep the 'I' out of all contexts. We have need, perhaps, of the sophisticated innocence of Zen in order to laugh out of court the resultant manifold and complex absurdities of our ways of living.

And there is some ground for hope. No culture can be without its myths. It will necessarily be unaware of these—and by the same token, they cannot be manufactured. For our myths bear the burden of what is unexplainable in the premises of any culture—and there will always be the unexplainable. It is the sheer poverty, then, of the myths of a Self-dominated culture that is now daily coming to light: the failure of its arrogant gods. The myth of 'growth', for instance, as of some self-evident good, is now ever more sceptically viewed. And on a more mundane level, the myth of the 'English countryside' is revealed ever more nakedly as the self-

interested fabrication it so often is—as if it were not a compound of primogeniture and the Enclosures, to say nothing of
deforestation by our Neolithic forebears.

Yet as old myths die, new ones arise. And this substitution
can happen in the twinkling of an eye: not deterministically,
but in response to unfathomable longings and to sustain
humankind's best hopes for itself. Perhaps, then (just perhaps),
the time is coming for the sustaining myth of a humanity
seeking to make a lasting home for itself on this planet to be
that of community. Self, if construed as implicate to community, is likely to prove to be as 'real' as could be expected.

And this returns us to the question of scale. A conflict
between opposing metaphysics, waged on a scale and with the
weapons created by their ill-founded 'knowledge', could yet
see the end of us all.

Chapter Three

A New Politics

Greening of the Government

TOWARDS THE END of 1988 Margaret Thatcher, in a surprising speech against the general trend of her Government's policies, showed she had become aware of the dangers of climatic change inherent in the freedom she was otherwise pursuing.

Nobody likes their clothes being stolen: it leaves them feeling cold and naked. It is tempting, therefore, to mock at Mrs Thatcher's amazing conversion to a concern for Green issues. For was this not the same Administration which abolished grants for the conservation of energy in people's homes? The Administration of the technological fix? The Administration associated worldwide with the sovereign power of unhampered individualism? Yet it would be a mistake to write off Mrs Thatcher's conversion as a move to hijack the Green bandwagon. The alternative scenario is that on this bandwagon we might all start feeling a little less cold and naked.

For one thing, the whole Green movement must have heaved a collective sigh of relief that the inevitable has been averted: that the catastrophe lying at the end of our present way of life has at least been recognized, and that some modification of that course is now not unimaginable. And secondly, the signs are that Mrs Thatcher has not—as have some other party leaders in the past, from time to time simply borrowed the clichés of the Green movement, but rather has used her own language. To say, as she has done, that we may unwittingly have embarked on an experiment that puts our planet at risk may seem naïve, and even nauseating. (What 'experiment', after all: the unleashing of greed?) But at least it betrays her own thinking. It is not skin deep.

At this point, it must be said, we should all be the more grateful for this conversion in light of the subsequent release of the Meteorological Office's exhaustive research into the greenhouse effect, giving a result at the very top end of all previous guesswork as to the heating up of the world's atmosphere fifty years from now. The consequences of this would spell disaster for far more than all coastal cities: the climatic effects would indiscriminately ravage each and every one of the world's civilizations. There is, however, no reason to suspect collusion between Mrs Thatcher's speech and this later authoritative report. I would only say the speech has come just in time.

By the same token, I myself would give Mrs Thatcher the benefit of the doubt that her conversion was not simply a form of special pleading for persistence with the development of nuclear power. Admittedly, this side effect was explicitly in her mind. Moreover, she is faced, when it comes to privatization of the electricity industry, with rejection by her hitherto omnipotent market (which 'cannot be bucked') of the economics of nuclear power in a way to which she cannot be impervious as previously governments have been impervious to the reasoned arguments of objectors at two grand-scale Inquiries: Windscale and Sizewell. Nevertheless, to admit of a special case, even one as portentous as nuclear power, would be to put at risk a far greater principle; and I for one do not think Mrs Thatcher is so stupid as to have taken such a blind risk. Until this uncertainty about the degree of her conversion is clarified, one is bound to note the depravity of the choice we might be offered: nuclear power, and in everything else the licence of greed.

However, come lately as she has done to environmental concern, it would only be charitable to accept that Mrs Thatcher has not thought very far into the implications of her conversion, and it is at this point that it would be right to reserve judgement. Indeed, it is at this point that the well-known differences between Greens themselves—between the 'fundis' and the 'realos' in Germany, for instance—might find themselves touched upon. For it is not only by coincidence that Mrs Thatcher has simultaneously started to talk about the moral obligations of wealth in our society, nor that she is suddenly introducing concepts like 'citizenship' and 'community' into the political debate.

So the question arises as to whether this is realistic: whether, for instance, by any reckoning these abstractions could produce adequate props for a civilization threatened by the scenario implicit in the Met Office's report. To paraphrase from the Labour side of the political fence: how do you persuade the bloke with a villa in Marbella that he owes the community a debt?

One cannot but doubt if Mrs Thatcher knows how deep is the water into which she is venturing. To take only the question of the economics of nuclear power, even supposing ways could be found of forcing widespread use of this energy upon people, its major additional costs would not only be borne, say, in moving a car from A to B (probably through increases in fuel taxes), but far more so in the energy locked up in the production of that car itself. We are thus talking about fundamental changes in our accepted way of life.

Indeed, we are chucking the concept of 'growth' into the melting-pot. And in so doing we are bringing under scrutiny countless other apparently discrete economic relationships, yet all of which attest to the interdependence of each and all. How, for instance, is the ruin of British farmers to be avoided if EEC standards of nitrates in tap water are to be applied in Britain—and to privatized Water Boards, at that? Such questions could no doubt be approached piecemeal, but it would be unrealistic to suppose that the attitude in which they came to be addressed would bear any resemblance to what is now thought of as Thatcherism. Or is it possible, in this time of miracles, that she too might yet learn to see the world in a grain of sand?

That Mrs Thatcher should unwittingly have exposed cracks in her Government's philosophy should, however, have come as no surprise. They were there to be seen during her semi-public disagreement with that most arrogant of men, her Chancellor of the Exchequer. For their argument was not really about the mechanics of flexible exchange rates versus variations in interest rates. The argument, rather, was really occasioned by the failure of Thatcherism on the macro scale to match its achievements on the micro scale. That is to say, in getting government out of people's hair, the Thatcher Administration has been at a loss to know how to restrain the consequences of such freedom. Keynesian 'forced saving' through taxation is ideologically out, yet the parts of 'the economy' are not adding up to a whole. Providence has failed. To this macroeconomic problem of untamed individualism, then, Mrs Thatcher is now adding the megamacro problem of the environment. How her supporters must wish it were just an electoral ploy! But it isn't; the genie is now out of the bottle. In these circumstances, alas, it is all too easy to predict the Government's most likely course of action—we shall be forced to be Green!

The Economist, that joyless bastion of materialistic reaction, has shown its hand as a new-wave 'realo'. It recently summed up its supposedly hard-headed recipe for social realism in an incorrigibly materialistic society: "Individual responsibility plus collective efficiency: that is a better model for the next twenty years than the hope that good citizens will build caring communities." *Gesellschaft*, not *Gemeinschaft*: the corporate, not the communal—that is the last refuge of materialism, the person reduced to a cypher in the social machine. Napoleon could not have put it better himself. And very likely this is the desperate measure to which any future government of any nation state—not just Mrs Thatcher's—will resort. More centralization to counteract what centralization, the separation of person and world, has brought about. The mechanistic emptiness of it all! The sheer desperation of spirit! And the drug culture that will be needed to sustain it.

My purpose here is not to make prescriptions. It is only to say that Mrs Thatcher has now changed the agenda of politics— and not necessarily to her own advantage—more radically than by anything she has done in the past ten years. For this at least she deserves our gratitude. It remains to be seen whether those who call themselves 'Green' are equipped to meet the challenge. The future is in their hands, more than in the hands of Mrs Thatcher. Unlike her, they do not start with a contradiction.

The Fall and Rise of Green Politics

NOW, IN 1992, the Green tide is on the ebb; of that there is little doubt. Environmental programmes on television are a big switch-off; the Green Party is a laughing-stock; Rio is forgotten. Yet, presumably, the globe has not stopped warming up, and the disjointures in our society, even in terms of its own values—as, say, between inflation and unemployment—only grow worse. But what has gone wrong with the alternative?

Some say there has been a surfeit of gloom and doom. In their apparent helplessness to do anything, people want to hear no more about it. Whether this is so or not, it must be said this helplessness was part of the critique in the first place. People truly are helpless in face of the scale, abstraction and alienation of everyday experience. Recognition of this has underlain such a slogan of the alternative movement as 'Think globally, act locally'. Perhaps they persuade themselves this is what they are now doing when they buy goods that have a Green label on them. But, if so, this would only confirm that the Establishment has neutralized the Green movement. Green consumerism is as materialistic as any other sort; the possession of objects, whether Green or not, remains its ruling passion.

Others say about this ebbing tide that the media, in its neurotic search for novelty, is simply moving on to exploit the next fad, whatever this may be. In so far, then, as 'the environment' has been a media phenomenon, there may also be truth in this; but the sickness in the world which the Green movement aims to cure could not be better illustrated than by this level of unreality.

Others again say that the realities of economic depression have relegated environmental concerns to the sidelines, where they are to be seen as luxuries of the rich. But if this is so, it can only serve to show how profoundly misconceived these concerns have hitherto been.

THE ROOT of it all, indeed, is a misconception about environment. This misconception is built into the very manner of thought that has brought the world to all its environmental anxieties. The simplest illustration of this misconception is the very notion of 'the environment'. This is commonly taken to be another thing 'out there'; another object separated from the subject observing it. 'The environment', however, is nothing but a metaphysical fantasy: no such thing exists, or can exist, for if it did exist it would perforce do so in some other environment. Environment itself does not have the characteristics of a thing; it is not separate. It is just what makes possible the idea of a thing. This is not to say it lacks extension in time and space; but rather it has no reality of its own. We and our environment are inseparable.

The consequence of this metaphysic of 'the environment', however, is that we suppose it might, like anything else, be possessed and managed. This has fatal consequences, and leaves the real problems untouched.

As a constituent of our dualism, of our subject–object cast of thought, 'the environment' takes one of two forms. The first fits into the frame of Humanism. Not-in-my-back-yard

(NIMBY) environmentalism is perhaps the most blatant case of this form: the use (or misuse) of the notion of environment to protect the narrowest of self-interests. On a broader view, however, much that passes for environmental concern (and however nobly stated) is actually in the last analysis about the survival of humankind on this planet. (And this goes for the notion of 'sustainable development'. What does this mean in an entropic universe?) In this humanist frame, our concern for 'the environment' is really concern for ourselves.

Over and against this humanistic environmentalism, and on the other side of the duality, is what might be called environmentalism as an idealization of Nature. The idea of Nature has, of course, a long history in the West. Certainly St Augustine used it in laying the foundations of Christianity. He treated nature as the surrogate for an inscrutable God in order to determine the proper order of things, thus equating evil with the unnatural; and its increasing use in medieval times paved the way for Western science.

There is an inbuilt tension, however, between the concepts of Nature and of Man (or specifically of the Self), and has been ever since Adam and Eve put their clothes on, or Abraham cut off his foreskin.

In cultures such as Tibetan Buddhism, where the notion of Self as a substantial entity has no meaning, the concept of Nature, implicitly standing over against it as it does, is not to be found. In our own era, though, Nature has been celebrated by Romanticism, starting from the Noble Savage and going on to speak of "where every prospect pleases, and only Man is vile". Hence, today, romantic environmentalism may be more than tolerated when it is a question of saving the whales, say, but when it comes to 'leaving the countryside', by stacking poorer people up in cities, this romantic environmentalism discredits itself.

'The environment', then, whether in its Humanist or Romantic manifestation, contains the seeds of its own rejection. So it should not be surprising that people get bored with the discovery of just one more object, once its novelty has worn off. Nor is it surprising that, once an election campaign starts, it should be forgotten; for in a context of who should possess what—which is what our elections are largely about—'the environment' is clearly only of a lesser material-istic order. Consequently, everything is by now set to go on as before in the world as we know it. We shall be no closer to putting together again a world that we, in our search for knowledge, have dissected—without having given any thought whatsoever to whether that process was reversible.

What, then, is the reality of environment and what, if any-thing, can we do about it? One might say that environment is that wherein all relationships between identifiable entities occur: and without which, moreover, no such relationships could occur. Or equally one could say that all intentional rela-tionships have implications apart from those relationships themselves, and that they themselves occur in an environment consequent upon the intentional relationships of others.

Obviously we are talking (as well as we are able) not about the laboratory, in which particular things are isolated, but about the everyday quantum world in which everything is in relationship. And by the same token we are talking about a state of affairs—a climate, an atmosphere—in which one thing is indistinguishable from another; where, perhaps, the very concept of a separate thing has no relevance.

Perhaps, then, our original question could be better put: what has given the idea of environment such importance in recent times?

I suggest it has emerged as an antidote, not just to the rationalism on which our culture is founded, or even to the materialism attending this, but also to the desiccated intellec-tualism and the unfeeling positivism that now so imperils the world: in brief, to all that has followed the proclamation that 'I think, therefore I am.'

If this is so, the notion of environment carries a spiritual charge; for I would say that spirit (which is just as real as matter) resides in that realm where notions of causation, of inter-action between one object and another, can have no mean-ing. In Buddhism, in fact, this state is (perhaps regrettably) translated as 'Emptiness', and is the state which, in meditation, everyone may hope to attain. I would say then that, however unconsciously, the widespread resort of our times to the notion of environment is an invocation of Emptiness—or, if you like, to the spiritual core of all faiths, and of none—to fill the actual vacuum, the nihilism, of our materialistic culture.

If, however, as I am suggesting, environment is immune to intentional action on our part (if only because we inhabit an impenetrable mystery), can nothing be done about the offence it is increasingly causing us? An offence which is, at root, in the widest sense aesthetic, in the sense of an ugliness, an ethical impropriety of manifold kinds. Is environment, thus understood, merely a sanction for fatalism?

Surely not! There may be aspects of the unknown that are intrinsically unknowable, but the incidence upon us of this incomprehension, the area of our experience affected by it, is not fixed. This may seem a convoluted way of saying, simply, small is beautiful; for that is what it amounts to. The closer the actor is to the implications of his actions—the less his acts are governed by abstractions—the more diminished will the sep-aration be between the world and himself, and the less dual-istic his understanding of it.

Yet, admittedly, this gap can seldom, if ever, be fully closed. Our knowledge of all wholes is necessarily limited (cf. Wittgenstein: "The meaning of the world must lie outside the world."). That truth is what underlies the fallacy of all Utopias—Green or otherwise. In practice this simply means we can do no more than set in reverse the trend towards giantism that dualistic thought has engendered. Indeed, with no help from the Green movement, and as a matter of common sense, this trend is being reversed in any number of businesses today. But the political dimension of this trend is still missing (if one excepts the belated conversion to 'subsidiarity'); and of course it cannot be supplied within the logic of the Nation State, which is nothing but an instrument to exploit the power of 'knowledge', and hence itself a main agent of environmental degradation. So the Green movement needs a political dimension—but not of the sort it has had till now.

We should take a lesson from the early Christians—as our circumstances are not dissimilar. The gods of Rome were failing, just as an ineradicable doubt has now been planted in people's minds about the gods of materialism. The indifference of the early Christians to their rulers is matched by the growing contempt in which the 'political class' is held today. The Christians took no part in government, but by the time of Constantine they had become indispensable to it, and without them he could not have captured Rome.

In the same way, then, a policy of positive abstention from central government, combined with practical programmes of mutual help on the local scale, would be a logical development for the Green movement. This would be a politics of constitutional metamorphosis. But what should not find a place in any Green political programme, conversely, is any talk about managing the environment. That is not merely futile: it is sacrilege.

None of the foregoing should be taken to mean that either or both kinds of Green political alternative are to be despised. Either of them offers a better prospectus than the orthodoxy of present-day materialism; and the tension between them could at least define the politics of a future more tinged with Green. Nevertheless, the antimony of these competing alternatives no more than perpetuates the very fault line of our present frame of thought. What I want to say, rather, is that realization of a new paradigm—indeed, of a more abundant life—implies a much more profound change in our everyday lives than has been dreamt of by either kind of Green politics.

The Hidden Agenda

Ours is a culture so habituated to getting and spending, to possessions, that without a second thought we would appropriate what of nature no one can possess: I mean the environment, and therewith the politics of the environment. Herein lies the current debasement of the word 'environment'.

It might be said, perhaps, that the devaluation of a mere word is of small consequence. But there can be no guarantee that once this particular word was discarded another could be found to take its place. It is the very meaning that would be lost. And that would be terminal for our civilization.

It is through the notion of environment that in recent times, and perhaps intuitively, we have sought to counteract the loss of meaning attendant upon our fragmentation of the world as a means of mastering it. The environment stands against the atomization of the world into discrete objects, into supposedly substantial things, each thereby subject to our manipulation: 'environment' signifies a world of interdependent relationships, one that subsumes ourselves.

So how can there be a something, like the environment, that is a nothing so far as possession of it is concerned? Cannot all things, intrinsically, be possessed? This is not a question of supply and demand: not even about the air we breathe, for example. It is much more subtle. It concerns whether relationships can be possessed, and especially whether those who owe their existence to a relationship can take possession of it without destroying themselves in so doing.

This question is about a putative politics of the environment. In such a politics, who could claim the environment? Many already do—consider those who enjoy the privileges of the Green Belt! But should anyone do so? The environment, being an interdependence of relationships, is about wholes, about forms of life, not about a division of the spoils. So its politics can only be about an improvement, or a completion, of the whole.

Yet the Green Belt is not just a scandalous abuse, leading to the bottling up of the poor in inner cities: not just a mis-application of its original intention—which, taken romanti-cally from the Greeks, was to limit cities to a human scale, but which was applied in despair to modern urban growths already beyond redemption in that way—but is also a pointer to the self-interest of which all contemporary environmental-ism is becoming suspect. For, suddenly, we are frightened. The greenhouse effect concerns us, perhaps not so much for our-selves, and perhaps not even for our children's children, but rather for the goods we have laid in store for them.

Just how selfish is all this new concern for the environ-ment? And if this concern, with its piecemeal, sticking-plaster remedies for impending catastrophes, is lacking any sense of the spiritual meaning of the environment, then, it is fair to ask how genuine our interest in it can be!

Is this interest not just another excuse for our taking pos-session of the world? The reduction of nitrates in the soil, for instance, to conform to some hypothetical standards of purity in drinking water, does this really betray an interest in the bal-ance of nature? Or is it not entirely anthropocentric? Is not our supposed interest in the balance of nature only a short-hand for our interest in our way of life? Is not our opposition to the destruction of the rainforests just the other side of the coin to the self-interest of those who are doing it? Are we not as selfish in our concern as they?

Is not the environment, in other words, just another thing to which we would lay claim, rather than a means of atone-ment? The tone of our concern for it, at all events, is already dangerously far removed from, say, the nobility of the North American Indians' respect for the earth.

It follows from this thinking that a politics of the environ-ment is, in truth, not even a politics of altruism—the kind of politics, for instance, that Marxist Greens would want to pur-sue—a politics concerned that others should enjoy a better environment. This may seem harsh, but a politics of the environment is about the environment itself. It is certainly doubtful that one class of materialists would respect it more than another. What is just conceivable, nevertheless, is that there might be a politics of what makes for a good or bad environment; and such a politics would embrace the roles people should play in it.

Such a politics would be, in the broadest sense of the term, a politics of aesthetics: of the seemliness, let us say, of our forms of life. And it is not unknown for such a politics of the environment to be practised. It has, after all, been the role—virtually the only role—of the Japanese Imperial family for nearly a thousand years to engage in such a politics. It is, moreover, a role the Prince of Wales seems to be taking in Britain. You don't refer to prestigious buildings in the capital as "a glass stump", or "a carbuncle on the face of a well-loved friend", without posing a silent question about the whole development process and the values underlying it that have produced your objects of scorn. Other countries, such as France, have long since practised the politics of culture. Nevertheless, the transposition of the politics of self-interest into a politics of the aesthetic, if it is not to fall into absurdity, begs many questions.

OF COURSE, it might be claimed that a politics of the environment could be one as between, let us say, environmental minimalists and maximalists: of those whose selfish interests were least and most limited by environmental concern. Or, put conversely, those whose environmental concern was most or least corrupted by, say, the not-in-my-backyard syndrome.

There is no logical mix, however, between a politics of special interests, such as we now experience, and one of the environment; they are as oil and water. A politics of gain could not accord the environment the priority which our condition demands.

You can't start an environmental politics from a politics of possession by modifying the latter by a bit of action here and there; you can only start it from an environmental position, modifying this as need be to accommodate special interests.

The political units we now operate—basically the nation state—could not be applicable to a politics of the environment. Nor should this be surprising, for the nation state is one of the numerous concomitants of our flawed way of making sense of the world: of carving it up. *Prima facie*, if the environment is not an expression of self-interest by any component of it, but rather is such that these interests become only residual to it, its politics could not be conducted in large units, such as are nation states. The wholeness intrinsic to the notion of environment must be dissipated by the multiplicity of interests that any large political unit necessarily engenders.

Yet here we would seem to run into the problem that the environment is all-embracing, that the environment is the summation of all things. However, the environment is not about things—it is not the product of our automatic, Western reification of concepts. The environment, it might be said, is but an interdependence of phenomena such as enables us to be in the world as it is.

But by 'the world' is not here implied the totality of objects, for might not the world be seen in a grain of sand? Rather, it bespeaks the forms in terms of which we conduct life's business, yet all of which, when we see through them to the world as it is—when, like that greatest of Christian mystics, Meister Eckhart, we even say "I pray to God to rid me of God"—they are, in the Buddhist term, ultimately, though pregnantly, void. That, it seems to me, is the quality of the environment, and that is why the hidden agenda of its politics is a spiritual one.

Yet, if this is to say that there is not one environment but many, and that by 'environment' we are not talking about everything apart from ourselves so much as about a way of understanding the world, nevertheless it may leave a puzzle as to how each application of such a way of understanding could be isolated from every other instance of it. Is not one environment, thus understood, one form of life, interdependent with all others?

And if so, how can we speak of any one such as a whole? This puzzle should respond to recognition that the world as a whole is inconceivable: there is always some unproven assumption about that conception. "The meaning of the world", as Wittgenstein said, "is outside the world"; and this also lay behind his speaking, so enigmatically, of "limited wholes". A limited whole takes us to the limits of our comprehension about it; when all the explanations have been exhausted about why, say, a town is not a city, or another town, "my spade is turned", and we are left with a form of life.

Now limited wholeness does not preclude interchange between one whole and another: an environment is not a cocoon. We are all neighbours: a politics of the environment is inherently good-neighbourly.

We are in a practical sense, for instance, neighbours of those who today are cutting down the tropical rainforests, in doing which they are ravishing the Earth as the Americans did the Plains, or as our forefathers did, who deforested Britain.

So what would a politics of the environment dictate in this situation? Surely, either that we should plant trees to compensate for those that are being cut down elsewhere, or that, out of our profits, we have an obligation to pay for their cutting down to stop; or a combination of both. How else should we act, if we are to do as we were once enjoined: "You shall love your neighbour as yourself"?

OF COURSE, if an environmental politics can only be conducted in a framework of essentially local units, it would immediately seem to be at odds with the large scale of contemporary technology. Aside, however, from the fact that much new technology is exceptionally conducive to small-scale operation, it is a moot point as to whether an environmental politics of small units would not be more effective than one dictated by some world-scale authority.

Indeed, that point itself is scarcely moot at all, if it be accepted that co-operation is an indispensable ingredient of any environmental politics. What has to be asked, rather, is whether any large-scale of government (or anything else) is not inherently pollutant—and therefore self-defeating—because of the factionalism to which it will be prone and the various self-interests by which it will be ruled.

I can see two conditions in which an environmental politics might come about: an economic earthquake and an environmental catastrophe. It is now increasingly common knowledge that we are on the edge of both of these, and in conjunction. Should we be struck by them—as it is only in the logic of our practices that we shall be—I hope that, as they inevitably diminish our selfishness, there will be some, and an increasing number, who will say that the remedy does not lie in more medicine of the old sort, more corporate centralism, but in a politics that springs from a different spirit.

Chapter Four

Some Practicalities

Town and Country
(from a Buddhist Perspective)

LEWIS MUMFORD has written of how it was that when
the clocks first chimed the hours across the fields from the
belfries of medieval churches, human minds began to change.
Certainly, those churches had been founded to convey a different sort of message; and even today, by contrast, there are
still no clocks in the minarets of Islam—just the call to prayer,
five times a day (though nowadays, admittedly, often pre-
recorded). Even late in the eighteenth century Adam Smith
could authoritatively write that the use of a watch was, say,
simply to ensure you kept your appointment with Mr X, not
to keep time with time itself. But now even country people
are so busy with so many things, all regulated by the hours,
that the churches have become little more than part of the
scenery of the countryside. The clocks Mumford spoke of
were tolling a knell for the hosts in which they are placed.

The question underlying these remarks is, then: what really
is the distinction between rural and urban values, if any? The
question is an immemorial one in our culture; it goes back at
least to the ancient Greeks. For them, those beyond the city
walls were barbarians, and there Pan reigned, the god of unrea-
son, who in the Orphic religion had been expelled from
Olympus. It would be hard to contend that this bias is not still

with us. After all, the walls of Paris were only dismantled after 1870—and metaphorically, some would say, they are still there. The dissection of time and space into discrete units has allowed the cultivation of knowledge reductionistically by those who themselves were apart from, and protected from, the wild. The kind of personality living under such influence could hardly fail to differ from those outside it.

But that was then: history. What is left of it? In quite recent times the tide of humanity seemingly has turned from city back to country, and as dramatically as once it flowed the other way. Yet is it the same 'country', or the same 'city'? Do we not all watch the same television, consume the same pap, and therefore hold the same values? And is it not essentially the cities that have triumphed, and where these all originate? Besides, suburbia has superseded the old taxonomy of town and country, except in the nostalgia of a few; a few, nevertheless, whose values remain influential, making of suburbia a kind of no-man's land. In brief, it is the formlessness of our very ways of life that has become their predominant characteristic—and a main source of our gross perplexities.

For why should the forms of life concern us? Because, surely, it is with them that we always reach the manifold and inevitable ends of our understanding. In so doing we may become at peace with ourselves. So if there is formlessness about the places where we live, we become unsure of our own identity. Like Descartes, we then launch into the naïve process of discovering our own existence: we exist because we think about our existence. But therein lies the risk of the dualistic pursuit of knowledge: the risk that, in the process of a subject reducing and isolating an object, the Self will be corrupted by the imperfection, the incompleteness, of what it has isolated, and I, that Self, will no longer be aware of what I am—and will be aware only of my unawareness. Thus my life will be meaningless.

To somehow contrive an identity, therefore, will become a prerequisite of knowledge. Is this not why, in our so individualistic day and age, fashion and conformity to it has become of such pre-eminent importance—indeed, 'reality' itself—and yet is so empty? (St Paul also said of the Athenians that they were "forever seeking after some new thing".)

Fashion, it could fairly be said, is primarily an urban phenomenon and a function of youth. The city bestows upon such persons a kind of identity. Yet how ephemeral it is! It quickly dissolves into suburbia, and beyond. (Manchester, for instance, is now half as populous as once it was.) How else, moreover, is one to comprehend the phenomenal growth of the Third World cities? Not surely, as is conventionally assumed, by the lure of their prosperity. Anyone who has witnessed the squalor of Calcutta or Bombay—or, conversely, the bucolic values of a Bengali village—must feel at least sceptical of this materialistic assumption. Is it not possible, rather, that knowledge itself is the lure: this other kind of knowledge that will be yielded up by an identity with the city?

Hypothetically, then, it is tempting to say—and to say it unquestionably—that urban values are concerned with the pursuit and possession of discrete objects, with things that can be quantified, and by whose growth we can measure ourselves. Whereas rural values are to do with the ways of life and their relationships, and with what is qualitative, and with where we belong.

Perhaps there would be truth in such generalizations, though not because one would somehow be dealing with the essences of things: rather, because we would be dealing with the figures of speech of a coherent metaphysical system. To continue with their use, however, would now be worse than perpetuating a metaphysical confusion—for 'cities' have certainly undergone structural change, and 'rural' life today is unrecognizable from what it was even fifty years ago: rather, it would be to sanction the dualistic knowledge that has fed upon the miseries of these false identities, of the urban and rural. It is such knowledge that is dangerous.

So much being said, none the less, it should not be hidden that it is primarily the cities where the greatest harm has been done. Yes! I do not ignore that it was presumably of the country Hobbes was thinking when he said life was "nasty, brutish and short", nor do I think Marx lacked a point when he spoke of "the idiocy of rural life". But the fragmentation and manipulation of the world, which are the outcome and fulfilment of Descartes' purpose that we should become "the Lords and Masters of Nature", have had their cost in the sickness of ourselves, the pensive observers of it. And the most overt symptom of this sickness is the sprawling suburbia of cities that deprives each of us of our identity.

Now the tragic core of this situation is that we lack what we should not need to crave. In truth, it is to speak automatically from the Western paradigm of ideas. The source of our craving for identity is the kind of knowledge we seek. ("Knowledge itself is power", said Bacon.) Of course, Descartes is not solely to blame for this. To trace it back no further, it is observable by the fourteenth century, after the Black Death, in the lord's withdrawal to his private quarters from the common life of the Hall. And its roots surely go far deeper, into the cultivation of the soul in the Christian world. Even so, and with due caution, I think it would be fair to say that it is the rural pole of the contemporary dialectic of town and country which comes closest to the alternative form of knowledge to the dualism by which we have been swayed: that is, to holism.

Holistic knowledge has one prerequisite: that is, smallness of scale. To comprehend any situation—and it is about situations, not things—such knowledge must be accessible as a whole to whomsoever would acquire it, and this must limit its reach. By the same token, the acquirer of such knowledge is but part of the situation of which the knowledge is acquired. Naturally, however, such knowledge is of the feelings as well as the intellect. "The heart has its reasons that reason knows not of." Of course, not everything can ever be known about anything—but we are not talking about things. We are talking, rather, about situations in which the Self has no independent existence. In these circumstances, the question of identity doesn't arise—except, perhaps compassionately, as some kind of metaphysical comforter.

It might be thought, then, this takes us back neither to town nor country but, of all places, to our despised suburbia. Well, almost—but not quite! For, after all, suburbia is not only quite a mess and a sheer inconvenience; it is also very large—so large that it quells the spirit. That is to say, it is incomprehensible—not mysteriously so, but just needlessly so. Our suburbs, in other words, need to be re-formed: or, to use an old-fashioned word, planned. Arguably, in fact, that should now became the prime focus of planning itself.

As a sort of Addendum, similar considerations apply to the so-called 'countryside', though perhaps with contrary physical effects. How, for instance, can the sacrosanct concept of the 'village envelope' be sustained against the increasingly probable permanent decline of agriculture as we have come to think of it? Does the resultant wilderness need to be protected as farmland was? And yet the demand—craving, even—for small plots of land is great: what if it is only for horseyculture? And perhaps Britain should be gardened as much as farmed—in which case the implications for village (and hamlet) structure would be immense. Villages prior to the Enclosures, after all, were very much more open than they now are, before agricultural technology implanted in people's minds the metaphysics of a need for identity.

In no way is this making a plea for chaos in place of order: simply for different forms of rural life. To know and help one's neighbours it is not necessary to live cheek-by-jowl with them, or even to do the same things as them on the striking of the hours.

Elmhirst and Rural Life

At the last, and shortly before he left the shores of Britain to settle in America, all too soon to die there, my father-in-law Leonard Elmhirst's energies were concentrated upon the completion of a project very personal to himself. Those energies, in his late seventies, were still remarkable and, as I followed in the wake of his negotiations, I could only marvel at them. They needed to be remarkable, however, for he was forcing his will upon the ancient University of Oxford. He was resolved to bring about the amalgamation of two of its component bodies. One of these—the larger and more prestigious—was the Oxford Institute of Agricultural Economics, then headed by Colin Clark, an economist of international reputation: the other, the minuscule (in fact the smallest component of the whole University) Oxford Institute of Agrarian Affairs.

Note the difference in their titles! The one was concentrated upon a narrow field of knowledge, yet carried much intellectual weight. The other covered a wide field yet had but small acceptance. It was with the latter that Leonard's concern lay. He had founded it and sustained it, and had somehow prevailed upon the University to incorporate it. Of late, however, his Institute, constrained by its small resources, had became little more than the Secretariat for the International Conference of Agricultural Economists, which Leonard himself had been instrumental in founding, back in the 1930s.

As such, the Oxford Institute of Agrarian Affairs still fulfilled an invaluable role—organizing worldwide Conferences and publishing their proceedings. The International Conference, indeed, from the start took an 'agrarian' view of its field: and its economists had muddy boots, knew what it meant to farm, and recognized that farming was meaningless outside an agrarian context. Yet, by the time in question, that was already a losing battle. Economics, pure and simple, was by then rampant in the academic field. The fashion was for econometrics, and agricultural economics followed in its train. I can vouch that Leonard

Elmhirst was saddened, if not defeated, by this trend of thought. It is small consolation that he would have felt vindicated by the disrepute this kind of economics has now brought upon itself.

He at least achieved his aim at Oxford. The two bodies were united, symbolically under one roof: Dartington House, provided by the Dartington Hall Trust. Leonard had successfully played the University at its own Byzantine game. And when, with Colin Clark's retirement shortly thereafter, Professor Ken Hunt of the Institute of Agrarian Affairs was appointed head of the joint Institutes, Leonard's scheme of things seemed fulfilled.

Yet (Professor Hunt's untimely death, shortly thereafter, aside) I think Leonard knew he had won a pyrrhic victory. He knew, I think, that without amalgamation the Institute of Agrarian Affairs could not have survived, and I think he must also have known its very approach to knowledge was doomed within the University. I suspect he was driven as much by a sense of responsibility towards those he had involved in his dream, as by any sense of completing his mission. Before he left Britain's shores, and the shores of life, he just wanted to meet his responsibilities as others saw them.

In thus closing his own book, however, Leonard Elmhirst left unexplained the springs of his beliefs. He professed no creed, though he was amongst the wisest of men—and it was part of his wisdom that he left Dartington Hall Trust no tablets of stone. You must remember, however, he stemmed from the West, and perhaps when he was perplexed it was only natural he should turn to Western values: to the supposed 'realism' of material things. Yet I think he only ever did so reluctantly and when he felt quite alone—and he must often have felt alone, surrounded by experts, specialists and professionals as he was. For it was not rationalism that animated him, but intuition: his feelings. And his intuition opened him to the wholeness of things: to the forms of life. I think his experience in the East* sustained him in this approach

---

* Leonard Elmhirst spent a number of years working with Rabindranath Tagore in India.

through all the travails of his creative work, and singled him out for the remarkable person he was amongst us.

Yet, of course, like us all he was often perplexed, and so in practice he was a rich mixture of East and West. (By 'East' I have particularly in mind the non-dualism of the Buddhist world and by 'West' I refer to the mechanistic universe of Newton's Great Architect. Perhaps it is India's special destiny to lie somewhere between the two.)

In the West, our idea of knowledge is to take things to bits to see how they work, to find some order in them. With one part of him, Leonard Elmhirst subscribed to this view. He was, for instance, a pioneer of artificial insemination in Britain, and of soil analysis, and he applied technology to the land in every possible way. He knew, however (as many others did not know), that in so doing he was tearing apart the fabric of rural life. Those others, I suppose, still put their trust in Providence, as their ancestors had done, to hold together what they had taken to bits. Providence, as we are now rather more aware, has somehow failed the West. I suspect, none the less, that Leonard also had some trust in it—otherwise he would not have been the child of his times, the squire of Dartington Hall and all that unchanging order, that he was—but he was also the possessor of two kinds of knowledge, not one. He knew inwardly, as well as outwardly.

In this I am referring to the epistemological crisis of our times: to the crisis about what knowledge is. I think this is central to an understanding of Elmhirst. Inward knowledge, I mean to say, comes from practice, from learning by doing, rather than by reflective thinking (one of Leonard's characteristic expressions was: "It has to be lived.") Being thus acquired, such knowledge is distinctive from that obtained by the dualism of observer and observed which typifies Western thought. This is best exemplified in the teachings of classical science. Hence, knowledge acquired by doing—by getting your boots dirty, or even by emptying the latrines—is not conducive to idealism, or Utopianism, for such constructs also oppose body to mind, appearance to reality.

Leonard Elmhirst was a pragmatist *par excellence*. In this, he took his cue from Thomas Jefferson, that great American champion of rural values, who, with Rabindranath Tagore, was the other main inspiration of Leonard's life. For Jefferson, America itself was an experiment, and that is how Leonard thought of Dartington: as the Dartington Experiment.

That explains, I think, why the Elmhirsts never built—or even considered building—a model village at Dartington, as several hundreds of well-meaning English gentry had done in the eighteenth and nineteenth centuries: 'well-meaning' in so far as those villages were the outcome of the enclosures of common lands for private profit. Nor was Leonard very interested in villages, as such. (I speak of his English experience. The English village has been highly romanticized, and is today all too often a hollow sham.) He was for many years a member of the Development Commission: a Government Department set up at the beginning of the twentieth century to cope with the problems of depopulation. The Development Commission did much good work. Out of it, for instance, grew the Forestry Commission, Fisheries Research, the Rural Industries Bureau (subsequently CoSIRA, the Council for Small Industries in Rural Areas), etc. But the Commission never looked at the forms of rural life (that is, at villages, hamlets, small towns) as such—as, for instance, planners must do. It looked only at their particulars, just as, indeed, Local Government in Britain looks only at services (like education, housing, roads, etc.) for local government is but the creature of central government. Indeed, rural decline has only been the other side of the coin of political centralization.

As a result, we have learned to our cost that those rural forms have become merely the functions of their services. Communities have been replaced by 'catchment areas'—so that when, for instance, some village school is closed in order to rationalize an education service, the village dies. Then, of course, we begin to worry—or rather, truth to tell, we are only now beginning to worry, because ironically today the English countryside is repopulating again, as the cities drain away! So, if it seems strange that Leonard Elmhirst was not concerned with this, if villages did not seem to matter to him—if, indeed, 'community' became almost a dirty word with him—well, you have to remember that, just as Jefferson had America as his world, so Leonard had his estate at Dartington, and this was world enough.

Dartington, one might say, was Leonard Elmhirst's ashram. This is not to say there was any sense of the hermitage about it. Perhaps the monastic tradition, out of which the English estates grew, is closer to the point, for the monasteries kept civilization alive, and were indeed the cradles of the Industrial Revolution.

Dartington, at least, was to be life as a whole, where head and heart and hand were to hold equal sway. The wholeness was, I think, intrinsic to Leonard's practice of learning by doing, and to his intuitiveness. That is why he at least recognized that technology of itself could tear the fabric of rural life asunder, and why its introduction must be accompanied by measures to repair that harm. For, of course, he believed in rural values. And rural values, I submit, have to do with ways of life as a whole, and hence with what is qualitative, and with the meaning of belonging. In contrast, urban values have to do with quantities, with the fragments that are reducible to what is measurable, with things rather than process and with 'doing your own thing' in the loneliness of the city. Between these two is a gulf which cannot be bridged, despite what sociologists would like us to believe, by suburban life, or any of the contemporary miracles of communications technology.

For Leonard Elmhirst, however, (given his belief in Providence) this wholeness of life consisted just in balancing one specialism with another . . . and with yet another, in all their profusion. If you say that this balancing must in the end beg the question of the context in which it all makes sense, I would agree. But I would say in Leonard's defence that the forms of rural life had ceased to exist (and still do not exist) in which a full life could truly be lived.

The village, by the twentieth century—and certainly after

the trauma of the Great War, which I think destroyed the spirit of rural England—had ceased to provide a vessel adequate to contain people's aspirations; perhaps because the Church, which was at the heart of the village, had lost its conviction. The congregation had become wiser of the world than the priest—and in 1916 Leonard himself abandoned the idea of entering the Ministry.

All the statutory services put together do not constitute a village. The countryside, I would therefore argue, must now evolve new forms to give meaning to the possibilities of modern technology. Without forms there is no meaning, and without meaning all our inventiveness, all our knowledge, and the material wealth it brings, are hollow.

At a deep level, is awareness of this truth that underlies the current repopulation of rural England: the realization that it is there that a worthwhile life might yet be lived. The explanation of this repopulation most certainly does not lie in the pursuit of material wealth. It is more to do, surely, with what it means to be a person.

There are mysterious undercurrents at work today. As animals know about the approaching storm before we do, or birds fly up before an earthquake, so people are fashioning a new way of life before the learned folk amongst us know what is happening. Seemingly, the search is on for new forms of rural life—and perhaps the search, the process, is more important than the end result.

Leonard Elmhirst was a pioneer of that search. His integrity was too great for him ever to proclaim he had accomplished it—at Dartington, or anywhere else. Like Tagore, who foresaw the danger of India simply exchanging brown masters for white, Leonard also eschewed simplistic political panaceas. He was wise enough to know you do not attain rural values simply by building a village, and perhaps that is true anywhere in the world. But I can tell you, as one who followed him at Dartington, that the search is at least an antidote to rural stagnation: Leonard Elmhirst's Dartington is still in process.

Pulse of Uncertainty

SCHOOL IS the institutionalization of dualism. After all, dualism is how we make sense of our lives: mind and body, the Self and the World, observer and observed, subject and object, etc. Dualism is indeed endemic in language—and we are trapped by language. Knowledge, or what in the West we take to be 'knowledge' comes from this dualism; through it we have mastered the natural world (or think we have). Schools, then, are places where we manipulate children as we manipulate the world, and where we impose knowledge upon them.

It is against this prologue that one must view the collapse of the education system, which we are seeing almost before our eyes. For what we are witnessing is much more than a mechanical breakdown in a system. Our dualistic way of understanding, of making sense of life, is itself in question, and this is inevitably manifested in the disaffection in our schools.

The sadness of this is that, after all, schools are the real world turned upside-down. In schools, knowledge is still knowledge, and curiosity still curiosity; knowledge is not the instrument of power over Nature (including over other people) it becomes in life. There it still a passage—albeit its rites are debased—from childhood to the adult state when the child leaves school for the 'outside world'; and, especially in some urban areas, schools still have a very necessary sheltering function. Yet the 'knowledge' in question is only the knowledge society recognizes as such, and which can be made to serve it. Ultimately, schools are not other than the world itself, and are held on its lease.

In speaking here of 'schools' one is, of course, thinking of orthodoxy. There are other kinds of schools, generally called 'progressive'. Their light has waned during the past fifty years. Simultaneously there has been a tremendous rise in popular, or State, education. No doubt great hopes were pinned upon the latter, hopes which progressive education had previously carried of serving some other purpose than orthodox schooling and particularly other than its proconsular pretensions. The new orthodoxy, however, was but social engineering writ large, not a substitute for progressive education at all—and several decades have been wasted in this confusion. For progressive education, classically understood, is not about knowledge but, rather, about the knower: about the person as a person, the child as a child, and his or her development.

Here we have the very nub of dualism. To explain: the progenitor of progressive education in our times was Rousseau, the father of the Romantic Movement and the conceiver of 'Natural Man'. To the intellectuals of the post-war orthodoxy in education—the Comprehensive School movement—Rousseau was, if not unheard of, almost a figure of fun. None the less, it is worth savouring some of the flavour of his *Emile*, if only because it is still more truly radical than anything dreamed of by those post-war social engineers. For instance:

Childhood is the sleep of reason.

Childhood has its own ways of seeing, thinking and feeling.

They are always looking for the man in the child, without considering what he is before he becomes a man.

What a poor sort of foresight to make a child wretched in the present with the more or less doubtful hope of making him happy at some future day.

Every state, every station in life, has a perfection of its own.

Reading is the curse of childhood . . . When I thus get rid of children's lessons I get rid of the chief cause of their sorrow.

Work or play are all one to him, his games are his work, he knows no difference.

You must make your choice between the man and the citizen, you cannot train both.

Let him know nothing because you have told him, but because he has learnt it himself.

When he fancies himself as a workman, he is becoming a philosopher.

Alas, all that richness went out of the window when the new social engineering moved in. The content of education became the academic curriculum, with its division of knowledge into 'subjects'—specialisms, for taming the world.

Our dualism of mind and body, then, has its most pregnant—even religious—manifestation in that distinction of which each of us is surely aware: the distinction between ourselves and the universe we inhabit. Language, after all, virtually imposes this distinction upon us by its subject-object relationships, and, in so doing, is the predicate of God, whereby that division is to be reconciled under Providence. "God would not deceive us", said Descartes of the gap his logic posited between the Self and that about which it thought.

Since education is about the knowledge we have of the world, this profound aspect of our human condition, its dualism, is bound to be reflected in it. In truth, not only Rousseau but nearly all the philosophers of education, both before and since him, have stressed the individuality of the child—whilst, just as consistently, the practitioners in the schools have stressed the importance of the world.

Yet the fact is that progressive and orthodox education exist in a symbiotic relationship. That is why progressive education was, characteristically, so reactive against orthodoxy. And it is why, nowadays, the decay of mass education has not been accompanied by the triumph of the progressive minority. Both are outworn. The malady goes deeper than education itself.

Now let it be clear, this is not simply to say that we must escape from dualism. Indeed, the root of the trouble might better be diagnosed as the belief of either party to our dualistic life—those who serve God, or those who serve Caesar: those who would abjure, or those who would master, the world—that theirs is the sole course to follow. This, alas, is as true of those who, following in the wake of John Dewey, believe in 'learning by doing', as of those who teach reflective knowledge from books.

Learning by doing, for sure, provides a very real kind of knowledge: inner knowledge, comparable perhaps to the gnosticism of old, and like it, it focuses upon the doer, upon him who has this knowledge (upon Rousseau's workman who is becoming a philosopher). Yet we must beware of escaping from the servitude of pedagogues to that of materialists. 'Doing', by taking part in the world's business, is not necessarily educative. The fact is that so long as we have language, we cannot actually escape from dualism. We can only mitigate its effects.

What we can do, rather, is to be aware of our condition. Now, to be aware of our condition is to recognize that when we are concerned with the person, we cannot know about the world, and when we learn about the world, we cannot know about the person. Life, in other words, is a kind of pulse: the pulse of uncertainty.

Thus conceived, life is less vulnerable to our immemorial passion to unify that which humanity has itself divided. This is a passion which can destroy the delicate balance between subject and object on which knowledge in our civilization hinges, and which, if lost, from time to time results either in ideological tyranny or in solipsistic anarchy. The pulse of the life we lead, for all its uncertainties, calls for the stability of various forms to be established if any meaning is to be found in it. In fact, the accusation to be laid against the monolithic, quantitative bias of our test-ridden schools today is that it is bringing us to a formless Age, fragmented and meaningless. No wonder "Things fall apart, the centre cannot hold", or that the authority of the teachers' certitudes is falling into contempt!

Schools in this analysis should perhaps not be necessary. As it is, however, they are an admission of society's failure;

they are the surrogates of community. We do not have a society in which schools could be dispensed with, because we have lost (or all but lost) the communities a child would need in order for the knowledge he acquires to be made meaningful. (Conversely, we have a growing store of meaningless knowledge.) Interestingly, Rousseau chose Emile from an aristocratic family, rather than a child of the lower orders, because his highly artificial background made Emile more in need of saving as a person. The lower classes, Rousseau thought, were closer to a natural life. Maybe! But when we have a whole world of bourgeois values, as now, how shall we learn from Nature?

That world does not any more exist in which to be a person is also compatible with, say, altruism. To be a person, today, is dangerously tantamount to being egocentric. Conversely, to not be selfish in a materialistic society is asking a great deal: to give of oneself (because, if it is anything, the Self is many-dimensional) in a world of quantitative values, must stretch credulity.

This rot has attacked the roots of progressive education also. What it means, surely, if paradoxically, is that we are entering one of those phases in history when the world itself, if any meaning is to be found in it, has to be created anew. Thus schools, if they are to have any validity, should perhaps set themselves to become a model for the world.

This is not as far-fetched as it might have sounded even a few years ago. With the world so estranged from young people on leaving school—and the ten-year-old son of one of my friends said to him the other day, "Daddy, what shall I do when I'm unemployed?"—schools are having to contrive a world of their own for young people: a world in which the Department of Employment, rather than the Department of Education, is having an increasing influence upon what passes for 'education'.

At all events, the opportunity is there for the taking, for schools to become more real than the 'real' world: of turning themselves into places where qualitative values hold sway, where inner as well as outer knowledge is cultivated, where wealth is as much environmental as private or discrete, where Nature is lived with rather than mastered: perhaps, most fundamentally, a world not obsessed with the Self and its salvation, which makes of the world its chattel. After all, the monasteries achieved something like this at a moment of history somewhat comparable to the present.

To draw this analogy, however, is almost as much as to admit how undesirable, even if practicable, it would be for our schools to make this transformation on their own. To be a model is not to be the thing itself. The hope should perhaps rather be that schools might be the catalysts of change: of change, that is, in their surrounding communities—or what should become their surrounding communities—such that between school and community there would come to be no perceptible difference. (At least the curriculum might then be determined by the community, rather than the community becoming, as now, the mere residue, the 'catchment area', of subject functions.) But of course this presumes huge social changes, and the reversal of trends towards the large and impersonal in scale going back over more than 200 years.

Yet it is not impossible. Between the hierarchical society of orthodox education and the anarchical society (so unnerving to some) of the true progressive school—in which Martin Buber's 'I–Thou' word necessarily obtains, in all its forlorn nobility—there must surely be another course. It is one that can only be made possible, however, in a community whose members themselves take responsibility for its children. For where this happens knowledge will have meaning and children will be manipulated no more than the community would manipulate itself.

The duality of our life would be inescapably present in such circumstances: the child would both grow as a child, for he would be known personally by his teachers, and he would acquire knowledge of the world. *Pace* Rousseau, he would became both man and citizen. But neither component would be enshrined in a principle, or institutionalized, to the exclusion of the other. The community, if it is to have any reality, would not allow of this. It is not, in the end, education that must change society, but society education, because education has no separate existence.

False Economy

The violent Stock Exchange crash of 1987, taking nearly everybody by surprise, was followed by economists turning their massive analytical powers on to whether or not this would be succeeded by a recession, and even by a depression as deep as 1931, which followed the only comparable Stock Market crash (at least in living memory), that of 1929. Predictably—and it is, as usual, the only predictable thing about this supposedly most scientific (i.e. mathematical) of the 'social' sciences—the economists' conclusions were at complete variance with one another. However, they had their excuse: apparently, it was all a matter of fine tuning!

That is to say, the economy had to be steered between the Scylla and Charybdis of inflation and recession. A little too much encouragement here and it would hit one rock, too little there and it would hit the other. Of course, this skilful steering would require a political consensus among those aboard the ship—the American trade/budget deficit, for instance, must respond to political treatment, and the Third World debtors mustn't rock the boat—but, by and large, people should respond rationally to applications of the usual economic forces.

People! What are 'people'—apart, that is, from being the plural of person? The notion of a person, however, is of something whole in itself, of the totality of a human being's values, attributes and properties: all that, in fact, makes for one's uniqueness in the world. But, just because of this uniqueness, one can't constitute the world itself of people—not without them ceasing to be 'people', and becoming merely the players of different roles in the world. And a person is not just the sum of his or her roles. The inner life of each of us would preclude that. So this is where alienation obtrudes itself: the notion, namely, that we may be playing roles in the world that are alien to ourselves as persons and, by the same token, at variance with what the world means to us. And one thing's for sure: that if there is such an entity as 'the economy' at all—and that remains to be discussed—it is shot through with alienation.

The notion that the economy is none the less something made up of 'people' can be dated from the introduction of Keynesian aggregates of his 'General Theory' in the late thirties: Gross National Product, etc., in which was gestated our subsequent enthralment by 'growth'. This marked the triumph of 'objective' economics over the subjective basis of classical economics in marginal utility theory; and, through the statistical depersonalization of its subjects, and their mechanistic interactions, it opened the door to the mathematical model-making, ever more remote from contact with the ordinary world, that has characterized economics ever since.

The trouble is that, though mathematics can be used to describe the natural world, molecules don't talk. But people do, and they act in terms of their language, which itself is inherently ambiguous. However, the long-term significance of the crisis in question may lie as much as anything in its challenge to the pretensions of economics—and Keynes knew very well of the potential conflict between full employment and inflation: would that he had only looked more deeply into it! What is perhaps of interest, rather, is whether what is nothing but a complex compound of alienations can in fact be stitched together by some preternatural agency to constitute an 'economy' at all.

It may be helpful to indicate the scope there is for alienation in 'the economy' by mentioning just a few of the con-
flicting roles in life which are ostensibly subject to economic
forces—a list albeit only in generic terms, most of which
could be multiplied scores of times: such as buyers, sellers,
workers, managers, shareholders, executives, spenders, savers,
proprietors, tenants, parents, teachers, students, thinkers, doers,
farmers, conservationists, voters, politicians, bureaucrats,
wives, husbands, vegetarians, drinkers, anglers, television
addicts, artists, technicians, craftsmen, scientists, entrepreneurs,
taxpayers, citizens, pensioners, professionals, laymen,
employed, unemployed, self-employed, trade-unionists,
adventurers, trustees, masters, servants . . .

The point of such a list is not that any one person has to
play one or other of the opposites of these roles (which he or
she doesn't), nor that some people can share an interest with
others in some roles but be opposed in others, nor even that
there has to be some uniformity about who shares or doesn't
share various interests. All of that can no doubt be taken care of
statistically by averaging out the reactions of everybody to any
given stimuli: like Keynes' concept of 'the propensity to save'.

The point, in the first place, is to suggest that in a pluralis-
tic society 'fine tuning' may be unpredictably hard to effect.
The more alienated a person feels from him/herself in whatever role society has prescribed—the more, in fact, someone is
just playing a role—the less amenable that person may prove
to policies idealistically taken in the name of society as a
whole. But in the second place, and more cogently, the list suggests the innumerable fractures along which the reactions to
any blanket stimuli could develop: the stress lines along which
Economic Man is reduced to a caprice.

Well, that can no doubt all still, with infinitely sensitive han-
dling, be taken care of (whether that were to entail still greater
alienations, or no) by some computerized version of the
Hidden Hand of the market. But what if alienation takes the
form of bewitchment by the figures of 'the economy' itself?

This could be of two types. Either there could be a mass hypnotism by 'growth'; and this, arguably, is what has happened in the United States, where the proportion of savings has already dropped to three per cent of income and is still falling (they must surely have taken leave of their senses, for whatever reason), leaving the rest of the world to finance their consumerist illusion—until, of course, the world refuses to do so. Or, alternatively, there could be a pervasive disgust about the figures of 'growth' as being ultimately empty, null, spiritually dead; and hence a rejection of the policies to which they are directed: a mass opting out of 'the economy'. There are indications, in fact, that West Germany is approaching that point. They seem, there, little interested in more 'growth': perhaps they'd rather go fishing? Yet, apparently, the salvation of the world from recession depends on their 'growing'. (The same is even more true of Japan, where, over a full decade of recession, people have simply failed to respond to the levers of control.) And, of course, the palpable nonsense of the Stock Market being determined by whether or not the indices reach some magic numerical level is all part of the same pathology. The measure determines what it shall measure.

Of course, the Hidden Hand of the market is itself in some disrepute after the Stock Market crash. In fact, the origins of that event can be adduced to its own kind of alienation: the separation of those who deal in money from the 'realities' of which money is supposedly the reflection. Or, in human terms, the alienation from oneself that greed can induce. There is also another alienation of some consequence to the world: namely, the separation structurally built into the U.S. Constitution between those who legislate and those who govern. But this doesn't help much, in the absence of Providence, to see things whole; nor when it comes to appeasing the Scylla of inflation.

It's true that these two major disabilities are alienations we have so far managed to survive without the world coming to an end. Likewise, the economics of aggregated human beings—the economics, in fact of 'the economy'—may for nearly half a century have papered over the cracks of a materialistic society, composed as it is of ever more discrete parts that no natural mercy holds together. But perhaps we're coming to the end of the line? And, if so, perhaps fine tuning, like a medicinal overdose, will only topple the equilibrium.

If we are at the end of the line, then, it is because the simplistic aggregates of economic policy will no longer serve to prevent things falling apart. That this may be so is because humanity is tacitly in revolt against being treated as if people were objects, the mere sum of their parts; and equally against the world being regarded as something to be plundered, rather than to live with. If this is so, it would doubtless be a waste of time to say to the Finance Ministers at the next meeting of the 'G7', presumptively as futile as the last: "You have a deeply flawed understanding of the meaning of human life." But would it not be true?

Grown-up Politics

THE *INDEPENDENT* newspaper, in a generally sympathetic editorial commenting on an opinion poll showing the astonishing extent of political support for the Greens in the European parliamentary elections, concluded, in a daring afterthought, "There is also a place for a spiritual Green movement, but as a religion, not a political philosophy."

One despairs of one's friends! Where is one to begin? Perhaps by referring them to the excellent article on 'The Hindu Heresy' in the July 1989 issue of *Resurgence*. That article spelt it out: that Hinduism is an invention of the West, of the West's compulsion to impute religious categories where none previously existed, in order to create the world in its own image. Because we have religion, so must they; and by 'religion' is understood all the paraphernalia that would treat of the spiritual as a separate way of life.

Yet perhaps that would be the wrong way to begin. It would require too much patient explanation of how the West has become unique in this respect, of separating God and Caesar. That would be to go to the roots. But our friends do not yet realize that they have to go to the roots. To do so would only be to lose their attention. Better to start by suggesting how a Green politics is nothing if not spiritual, and that there is no spirituality divorced from everyday relationships, even political ones.

A politics of the spirit is a politics of whatsoever is whole, not of parts of a whole. Since all wholes are limited, such a politics is one of uncertainty, rather than of ideological certainties. The spirit bloweth where it listeth. The wholes of a politics of the spirit are not utopias, fixed or unchanging.

A spiritual politics is not about the reduction into material shares of our abstract 'wealth': about who gets what. This is gross materialism, however disguised. It not only sells the pass to a debasement of wealth—to growth, and all the rest of it—but it casts aside the interdependence at the core of a politics of the spirit: interdependence that confounds our deterministic certitudes about the processes of causation in the midst of which we find ourselves.

By now, one's friends might be wondering where all this leads. For where it does not lead, it seems clear, is to what 'breaking the mould' has come to mean: that is, just to substituting some new party for another over all the contentions of the old. Maybe, not even the Greens! For those old contentions use a different language from the new, one with different meanings for words like 'wealth'. And the difficulty one's friends have with an enspirited politics is that it must take place at an unimaginable mental distance from the only politics they know. For it is clear that a Green politics could not be conducted in terms of the one unit that lends legitimacy to our current politics: namely, the nation state. There is nothing Green about a nation.

The politics of the nation state is but the sum of its parts. There may arguably be some common philosophy mediating the exigencies of each government department of today's nation state, but a nation, in all its contemporary size and cultural and technological complexity, is impossible to govern, except reductionistically. It's true that there is a certain unity in the idea of a nation itself, a certain wholeness, but, such as it is, it can only find expression in terms of power. It is only by power that it can be comprehended as a whole: that is, be consented to and given legitimacy.

Power, however, has its own rationale, and this excludes the manifold other dimensions of a nation's life. To comprehend a nation in terms of power is to not comprehend it in all the other ways of its life. How is Britain, say, to be understood in its fullness when there is no consensus even about what London is, or where it starts and ends? To say nothing of many a smaller place: for what has happened to our sense of place? How limited, indeed, is a politics based on the identity offered by power!

Now it might be contended that there is a yet deeper motivation than power underpinning the nation state: namely, our fear of uncertainty, our anxieties and our need for security. ours is a culture predicated on the pursuit of certainty. Even though our own science now tells us that the world is inherently uncertain, this craving for certainty is not to be despised. To contrive a scenario contrary to the recognized truth may be a testimony not so much to our perversity as to our weakness. Perhaps we cannot stand too much truth; our illusions matter too much.

Yet the power-centred logic of the nation state only makes matters worse for ourselves in these respects. The centralization to which it lends itself, like all repressions, only increases the uncertainties with which we must live. The more the state seeks to control the full spread of our activities, the less effective it will be, because the interests of the state are so much narrower than those of its subjects. It is amazing, for instance, that those intelligent people in Whitehall have not yet even questioned whether their centralized control over 'the economy' might not actually be the primary cause of its inflation.

The problem is to discover the political units which would allow us a bearable degree of uncertainty. How can we do justice to the interdependence of the components of any limited whole; to discover the environment in which political action makes sense? For the Green movement, the political question is a constitutional question and only a constitutional question: it is to change the ground from which the legitimacy of government derives. If necessary, a Green politics must continuously change this ground because such a politics is not goal-oriented: it is concerned with the sustainability of life and culture. The emerging mindset, of seeing things whole, will occasion its own fresh matrices.

I am talking of a revolution, you may think, but where are the revolutionaries whose interests are being served? The only interest being served in the establishment of environmentally viable political units is that of human self-preservation. The discovery of these units will be a messy, trial-and-error sort of affair. It will arise from disgust with the old dispensation.

This implies the renunciation of most of its powers by the nation state, and the adoption of these powers by much more local centres of government. This is the only plank of the Green Party programme that really matters. The change of mentality predicating all the rest of that programme must first be set in a new political paradigm. Of course, this is not to exclude manifold *ad hoc* agreements across the boundaries of these local governments; we are not talking in terms of some kind of New Age autarchy. Politically the world has to grow up; that is what the Green movement is trying to tell it. And this is a spiritual process.

Energy and Form

ANYONE WHO IS basically literate about energy (which is at most what I myself could claim) knows that the savings to be made by conservation are enormous. They are so enormous that *prima facie* they reduce the nuclear issue, given its terrible imponderables, almost to a non-question. Yet to make this large claim for conservation is, in itself, almost as facile as to hold that by one technological fix or another we shall get by the energy problem, as we get by all our problems.

I mean by this, simply, that we are not attuned to conserve; we are attuned to exploit. Indeed, we measure ourselves—our very purpose in life—by our capacity to use the Earth: by the growth we achieve from that use. Conservation, therefore is a matter of mentality, of our minds. We cannot be induced to conserve energy just because we know this can be done without lowering our standard of living, nor by price policies that would reduce its use, for our very idea of a standard of living requires that we spend energy to enhance it, and fiscal policies to constrain our exploitation of the world (rather than to raise revenue) would suffer under the same inhibitions.

I think it is here, perhaps surprisingly, that planning has its contribution to make. I mean by 'planning' what people understood by it before it became a dirty word. Planning means seeing things as a whole. And I am particularly thinking of town, or settlement, planning, with its premise that a town—or a city, or village—is more than the sum of its parts. Of course, that is not how planning has come to be thought of today. Nevertheless, it is how it first grew in modern times out of the Garden Cities movement.

Today, indeed, it has degenerated into bureaucratic negativity, and in a sense this was because its birth was premature. The language to nurture it had not then come into currency. Administrators like Evelyn Sharp in the post-war years emasculated it out of sheer incomprehension. The real tragedy

arising out of this is that planning's stance has been quite corrupted—such that those who should be its allies in the alternative movement regard it as their enemy.

Yet without planning (under whatever name) the alternative movement will be lost, for it will be without form. The
business of planning, properly understood, is with the forms
of settlements—whether towns, cities or villages. Without this
purpose, planning lacks all rationale. So too the alternative
movement, if it is to be more than a romantic conspiracy, must
find the right forms for its energies. The new paradigm itself
will drain into the sands if it is left formless, just as the old
paradigm is doing. Indeed, if I understand it aright, since the
new paradigm is to do with meaning—with the significance
of whatsoever we practise, rather than (as with the old) with
the knowledge we have—the forms life takes become
absolutely fundamental. For anything has meaning only in so
far as it conforms to some pattern; the whole confers meaning on the part.

This is why the language of planning is central to the new
paradigm, for it is the language of wholes. But this is only a
roundabout way of coming to the point: that the contemporary exploding city—formless and unplanned as it is—is a
prime case of profligacy in energy. Or, put differently, reduc-
tionist thought (the pattern of the present paradigm) is inherently wasteful of resources because the parts into which it splits
up the world are unconstrained, in their demands upon it, by
any pattern to which they need conform. There is no whole to
which they are responsible, and so they become meaningless.
Similarly, we have allowed our settlements simply to happen
because we have not learnt the language to create them.

The crisis of energy, in fact (as opposed to 'the energy crisis', which is largely a fiction), is a crisis in our way of understanding anything other than that for which money itself has
supplied the measure. The discrepancies between energy
accounting and financial accounting are indicative of this difference. And the crisis is a crisis because seemingly neither

people nor nature can much longer endure the way in which we depend upon money to make sense of the fragments to which we have reduced the world. Thus conservation depends upon our learning to speak the language of place and of community, of 'small is beautiful', and of the qualitative rather than the quantitative. It is a language we shall anyway be forced to speak when the last petrol pump attendant has been shot by some frustrated motorist.

The era of cheap energy greatly advanced the atomization of life and the disintegration of its forms. Yet this process was already under way and the motor car (for example) was only the instrument of the growing wealth which, in pursuit of private living space, turned suburbia into the exploded metropolis. The automobile has not really changed anything. It has only made the old, monocentric forms more incongruous.

Nor is it likely that the motor car will go away. The potential for saving energy in automobile design is so dramatic that it would be folly to plan any human settlement on the basis that the car will decline in importance, or even diminish in numbers. It is simplistic to suppose that public, rather than private, transport is the key to urban form. This could only apply theoretically if our purpose were to consolidate the antique pattern of settlements. It should be, rather, to change it.

The shock administered by the rising real cost of energy should at last make us comprehend the ongoing process of urban decentralization and give it form. Cities must become many-, not single-centred, allowing for the convenient proximity of all the functions of daily life. According to OECD figures, in North America with its gross urban sprawl the transport sector takes 34% of all energy consumed, in contrast to only 9% in a relatively car-less Eastern Europe. But the answer, surely, is not to go back to the congested and anonymous industrial cities of the past. It is, rather, to re-make the urban pattern. A sudden shortage of energy should shock us into recognizing the realities about changing urban form that have been present for generations.

SIMILAR PRINCIPLES apply to settlements in the country-side. Highly capital-intensive though it is, agriculture is ostensibly not a great user of energy. The direct use of energy, including fertilizers, is only about 5% of farmers' costs. The sequestered energy in farming's enormous machines is, however, a different matter, and points clearly to a less capital-intensive future for agriculture. It is not the petrol to put in the tank that matters, so much as the tank to put it in. England, one can reasonably argue, will have to be not so much farmed, as gardened—and by small-scale, family units: a complete reversal of current wisdom.

But it is not from agriculture, as a technology apart, that our examination should start, so much as from the context of rural life. More people, with more appropriate machinery, will need and want to live in the countryside—and the implications for its settlement pattern are as great as were the Enclosures. But without a new settlement pattern, these technical changes will be stultified. A certain kind of community is needed, after all, if England is to be gardened.

A stage beyond this is the question of community energy. If energy is indeed the currency of some new understanding of the world—which is to say, of what meanings life holds—we should expect it to play a central role in forming our communities. As things are, the alienation of the electricity grid and of all other kinds of energy that materialize from afar have been patent factors in the disintegration of our forms of settlement. They have cut the bonds of our dependence on each other. If, then, we consider not only the use of energy but how it is generated, it is conceivable that locally generated energy could play the most potent of roles in the formation of settlements.

To an extent, combined heat and power (CHP) schemes are the Establishment's death-bed repentance on this score. But presently received wisdom seems to be that CHP is only worth considering for communities of 100,000 or so. One suspects this may change, but in any case I am thinking rather of the potential of renewable energy sources. In this light, it seems possible that we shall increasingly witness the development of local energy plans, and that such plans could prove critical for the restoration of a sense of form in our lives.

It is, after all, this sense of form that is central to my argument. For (it may be said) it is all very well to contend that form should determine function, that our towns and villages, say, should not be the mere resultants of technology— whether of education, health, transport, sewerage, etc.—but the determinants of these provisions, such that there should be only appropriate technology. But what if our concepts of such forms themselves should suffer from illusions—say, from *folies de grandeur*? How, by according its proper priority to form, should we be sure of cutting our coat to the cloth of nature, so far as energy is concerned?

I think it is because form is integral to the new paradigm that we can be confident of this. Any form confers meaning upon its components, yet cannot itself be meaningful—except in so far as it is itself part of some pattern. (If something purports to be part of some form, yet lacks meaning, the validity of that form is in question.) Ultimately, we come to an end of explaining what something means in terms of the forms of which it is a part; not everything is to be explained.

But when that point is reached we shall want to feel that our forms of life are sustainable, that we are comfortable with that which cannot be explained. It is only if we are concerned with forms as such, rather than with the fragments of those forms in themselves, that this consideration will arise. And should we do violence to nature, I doubt if we could believe our forms of life were sustainable. We can already recognize our own arrogance towards the world in the discomfort we feel about continuing to live as we do.

For reasons of this sort, then, I think that if our use of energy were determined by the places where we lived, rather than determining these, we should find that we would cut our coats to the natural cloth of the world in terms of energy. I recognize that in all sorts of ways this would turn our lives upside-down, and that the thesis is untested. But must we not come to it?

The Great Questioning

"America's banks are not as healthy as they look."
—*The Economist* 10th July 1999

ANY GREAT questioning will begin when, and only when, the old truths are no longer self-evident. For us, this is not yet. For the moment, the old ways still stand—just! We still make sense of the world by exposing object to subject; that is, by dualistic thought, and we call it 'science'. True, the doubts are creeping in, not least in science itself, and particularly in quantum mathematics with its hypothesis of multiple universes. But it is not ideas that will change the world. Only events will do this.

So it is only when the fruits of the old thinking fail us that scales fall from our eyes; and, when next that happens to us, it can hardly be painless. For this change is unlikely to happen, for instance, through war or by reason of some foreign conquest, but, rather, in consequence of our own actions. The hardest thing to say, after all, is "Sorry!" So a great questioning, a questioning of itself by a whole society, will begin when the benefits that the old self-righteousness seem to have brought—whether of bread and circuses, or of our contemporary religion of consumption—have irrevocably crumbled.

For ourselves, moreover, if such a general questioning occurs, it will be made the more tortuous for happening in a moral vacuum. For in the years of our deceptive prosperity, which have recently accumulated by our making a virtue of greed, the immemorial virtues of integrity, unity, simple honesty and so forth have been all but lost. The solipsistic cast of our dualism has overshadowed its counterpart, the pseudo-objectivity of ideology—leaving us in a vacuum of nihilism. There is no more confidence in great systems of ideas. There can be no big solutions. And I doubt if an outbreak of goodness of heart alone will resolve our problems.

Nevertheless, it is not hard to envisage how an epochal change could occur, and anyone who experienced the 1930s

—the Great Depression—could tell you about it. Indeed, there has been a surprising amount of discussion about the 1930s. This has intimated that the turmoil in the financial markets has been something more than just another twitch in the system, of which there have been several over the past two decades. There is, some people feel, a deeper unease, and the unreality of the dizzying heights to which the American stock market subsequently recovered only lends credibility to it. It's all too like 1929 for comfort.

There is indeed growing reason to think that the volatility of the market is due precisely to the mathematical sophistication of the models to cushion risk that dealers have developed to counteract volatility. Certainly, the Dow Jones index of the top thirty shares is a dubious guide to the state of the American economy; the Russell 2000 index has still not recovered to the level it reached a year ago. Therein lies the rub: not with the Dow, however spurious it is, but with the very notion of 'the economy'. Supposing the economy itself were unreal, would there not be every reason for the nervousness of markets?

And the economy *is* unreal. What is it but a metaphysical construct? It is a product of the discipline of economics driven by the compulsions of measurement to conceive of a reification, 'the economy'.

To achieve this reification, economics had but to take to its blindly logical conclusion the abstraction of 'utility' upon which, as a human motivation, its early studies had harmlessly been founded. In so doing, it manufactured the object (the economy) predicated by our dualistic mode of thought, and having done so, it bewitched itself by measurements. But humankind has manifold other motivations than utility, none of which can be taken into the fabrications of economics. The metaphysical reification in question is thereby invalidated. One is tempted to recall the old joke: 'If all the economists in the world were laid end to end, they would not reach a conclusion.'

Measurement, indeed, is our hallucination, and money is its handmaid. Measurement gives us a false assurance of reality, but the money, by means of which economics peddles its theories, has an ever greater sense of irreality about it. Ultimately, in fact, our money stems from an international agreement in Basle (still not actually agreed) concerning the cover all banks should have on their loans, which create the 'money' in the international system. But since the quality of their loans could never be quantified, any formal discussion of the question would seem to be quite futile.

So it is money itself, as the proxy of value, which is a prime metaphysic of our dualistic mode of knowledge. Historically speaking, there is perhaps nothing derogatory about metaphysics. The great Victorian mathematical physicist Maxwell, whose equations paved the way for Einstein's Theory of Relativity, was very clear that metaphysics must set the bounds of Newtonian physics, and so it probably must. But it is another matter to transmute what's metaphysically useful into reality, as has happened in economics. It is seduced by the measurable qualities of money. Metaphysics, then, makes the world a dangerous place. The machine of the economy is all but programmed to break down.

The danger I particularly have in mind is of our capacity ever again to withstand anything comparable to the Great Depression: we are culturally enfeebled by our misuse of 'the market', and by our dependence on the measurability of truth which our dualism sanctions.

There are so many symptoms of this: the travesty of 'education' through instruction in subjects reductionistically defined and reified; the obscenity of the growing and condoned disparities of wealth and poverty; the misuse of science to pronounce on the environmental consequences science itself has generated; Europe absurdly traduced; our roads no sooner built than saturated; our feckless agriculture; our great cities at a loss what to do about their incurable suffering; in brief, our exhausted culture, its Golden Calves preserved in formaldehyde. But there is also a very real danger that all the disparate parts of this rootless culture will succumb to the collapse of their common metaphysic, the monetary system.

For the time being, the world's 'economy' is carried on America's back by means of its soaring balance of payments deficit. Americans themselves have ceased to save. Their houses are hugely mortgaged to the banks, the quality of whose loans is diluted beyond the bounds of normal prudence. And much of the cash thus raised is being used by individuals to 'gamble' on the internet, making up twenty-five per cent (and rising) of trading in shares. It is hardly a reassuring picture.

Yet, there is no telling when it will all collapse. All that is sure is that when and if it does, the aftermath will be catastrophic, with its attendant massive unemployment and loss of numerical wealth. The text-book devices to stimulate the fantasy economy would be as ineffectual as they were in the Great Depression, or as they have been recently in Japan—that is (heaven forbid!) in the absence of another quasi-Keynesian remedy like a World War coming to the rescue. More likely there would be sheer bewilderment. Japan's long-continuing depression is a portent of the probable failure of the usual mechanistic text-book policies to stimulate our fantasy of an economy.

Should this scenario seem far-fetched, it could be because disillusionment on such a scale is almost without precedent. Almost, but not quite. There is a hint of it in St Augustine's sorrowing over the sack of Rome. He, it is true, concealed that loss by building a Church in the city's image, and it may prove that only an equivalent spiritual charge will be able to compensate for the loss of the Golden Age of materialism through which we are now passing; but it would be folly to propose such a development. All it would seem safe to say is that our culture is but skin-deep. The state of our tabloid media is surely sufficient evidence of this.

In all this, in implicitly advancing the case for a smaller scale to our myriad activities, I might be accused of advocating some kind of anarchy. Well, I think anarchy has a noble pedigree, but that is not what I mean. I have in mind only a future in which interdependence and its values prevail, with the social structures endemic to such an holistic norm. I can only suppose these structures will be small in scale, rather than abstractly gigantic as now, if we are to apprehend the relationships between them.

Indeed, in the ultimate, where the world is recognized as constituted of the relationships of relationships, there would be no Self, nor any anarchists as such—but that perhaps is to venture into a distant territory, though one to which indeed a great questioning might lead.

As an addendum, let it be said that this challenge of the small to the large, however painfully it might be brought about, would be environmentally beneficial. 'The environment' is today in ever-increasing danger of being treated as just another thing, a figment of our dualistic thought, and hence of producing an equal and opposite reaction to our treatment of it. The preservation of the environment depends, if on anything, simply on how we live; and not on our idea of 'the environment'. The more we pursue theories by intellectual abstraction, the more we put ourselves at the mercy of the environment's incalculable storms. If there is anything still reliably predictable, it is the inadequacies of determinism.

In brief, then, at this juncture the American people should at least be made aware, as they spend their way into ever greater debt, that, should the fragile temple of their banking system fall in upon them, their world (and ours) would never again be the same. Of course, they won't listen; but later they might remember, and start questioning.

$$C=SN \frac{(\ln(S/K) + (r + \sigma^2/2)^t)}{\sigma\sqrt{t}} -Ke^{(-rt)} N \frac{(\ln(S/K) + (r + \sigma^2/2)^t -\sigma\sqrt{t})}{\sigma\sqrt{t}}$$

. . . or a Private Language

THE EQUATION ABOVE purports to measure the risks of investment. It served to win the Nobel Prize for economics for two American econometricians, who went on to became board members of the 'hedge fund' Long Term Capital Management (LTCM) which, in October 1998, had to be rescued by a consortium of banks put together in secret by the US Federal Reserve Bank. As events turned out—and in particular the fallout on the foreign exchanges of the collapse of the rouble—LTCM could not meet the debts of $200 billion (and perhaps more) it had risked against its own capital of $5 billion. The world's financial system and all the enterprises that hinge on it had come within a whisker of meltdown.

The LTCM equation, it should be said, is not exactly unique. There are many other 'hedge funds'—nobody can say how many, because they are inherently secretive. They certainly number in scores, and ostensibly they perform the sensible function of hedging one's guesses about the future of the market. Moreover, they presumably all use formulae of varying complexity to estimate the risks they run. LTCM, however, seems (hopefully) to be in a class of its own—the Nobel Prize class—in terms of both its size and its sophistication. It was not so much to do with anticipating the market as with speculating on others' anticipation of the market. The offspring was devouring its own progeny.

That this should have happened is the inexorable consequence of the bewitchment of economics by mathematics. This process has gathered speed with the acceptance of the Keynesian aggregates such as Gross National Product and the metaphysical and pernicious (as the European Union with its single currency will discover) notion of 'the economy' itself: all of these being built on the marginal valuations of 'classical' economics.

Before all this happened, economics had been a harmless and useless activity of teaching others to teach others economics. Subsequently, however, and over the past half-century, its new-found measurability of value has given economics the present status of a science. As the LTCM episode shows, it has also acquired some of the destructive potential of science itself.

This should not be taken as an attack on science as such; it is but to question the limits of its use. For what was most remarkable about the LTCM debacle was not so much the mathematical formula itself from which it stemmed, as its sheer incomprehensibility to all but a tiny group of initiates. The formula had, in effect, the secretiveness of a private language.

This is of the greatest interest because it was Wittgenstein's now classic demonstration of the impossibility of a private language—with its corollary that language is social, such that its meanings are never fixed and are not labels of the 'real' world—that struck at the heart of Descartes' idea of The Self and hence at the dualism of subject and object, the very notion of knowledge which governs the kind of world we have contrived for ourselves.

Furthermore, it is now forty years since a follower of Wittgenstein, Peter Winch, showed in *The Idea of a Social Science* that any inquiry into society can be pursued only in the language in which that society itself is conducted (or which could be intelligibly derived therefrom). Manifestly, this precludes any explanation of social behaviour in language derived from some logic outside it, and above all the application of any autonomous theory or ideology. In fact, all one can do is describe, not explain, how things are.

Nobody, of course, paid any attention to such ideas, and certainly not the economists. Their new-found powers of measurement were making them the arbiters of society—just as physics (pre quantum mechanics) was the arbiter of the natural world. What else was to be expected from a society in thrall to whatsoever was measurable?

Appropriately enough, the major exception to this indifference has been provided by that financial speculator *extraordinaire*, George Soros. In his recent book *The Crisis of Capitalism* he has openly expressed his disdain for the social sciences. Unfortunately, he does this on the somewhat superficial grounds that the behaviour of human beings is inherently unpredictable. People, in other words, can change their minds, not least when they are expected to observe any given laws of behaviour. He misses the deeper point: that social scientists are precisely restricted to the language of society, and this language is not one of abstract constructs but rather of life's ordinary language games. Nevertheless, it is encouraging to learn that this destroyer of economists has been guided in his business not by rational expectations, but by his intuitions.

Put another way, the board of LTCM thought it could play God with the market. This is what happens if you try to speak a private language, the truth of which is not verifiable except by reason of your own assertion of it. In practice, however, even if one holds a conversation with oneself—as we all constantly do—one must use public language to do so. Should we nevertheless persist in the construction of an inner world, the outcome can only be, at worst, madness of one kind or another, or sheer folly: which translates in a social context into something like another Great Depression—the last one of which required another madness, World War II, to transform it.

And maybe, from one perspective, we have been living in a war economy ever since 1939, a mere diversion from the Great Depression. At the time of writing, for sure, one can only wonder how much longer the rottenness of the Chinese banking system can remain concealed; and whether or not its collapse and subsequent devaluation will arrest any fragile recovery in Japan; and whether this will not plunge all southeast Asia back into recession; and whether the USA itself can indefinitely continue borrowing, through its soaring balance of payments deficit, to carry the world on its back; and whether Brazil will swallow the International Monetary

Fund's medicine, or collapse into inflation, and how that might affect the European banks to which it is indebted; and how many more of those banks are over-borrowed on more hedge funds; and whether the Euro, far from being a haven like the Deutschmark, will be politically manipulated, adulterated and shunned. All these are only tremors, though real enough. Yet they are all interconnected, and should even one of them crack, the world as we have known it would be but bits of paper blowing in the wind.

Should it come to this again, however, the next structural crash will not be like the last one: for since 1931 the values which then still provided some coherence to society have been greatly eroded. Who any longer believes in the simple virtues of honesty, loyalty, integrity, etc., etc.? That sort of fabric is shred and splintered. We live now in a Tabloid Culture, and there is no body to it. All our values would then be up for renewal: all our dependence on dualistic thought, of subject and object, of cause and effect, and all the social structures deriving from our rationalistic cast of mind. Nothing less!

It would truly be a time for resurgence, and we should be prepared for it.

There Is No Alternative

SOMETIMES I WISH my admired friends, the advocates of Alternative Economics, showed more knowledge of the real thing, economics itself. This is not out of *amour propre* on my part, due to my having in the mists of time taken an economics degree—an exercise in intellectual futility from which it took me twenty years to recover. The real reason, rather, emerges as one takes a deeper look at this thing called 'economics'.

There are two sorts of economics which give Alternative Economics its *raison d'être*. (I exclude Marxist Economics, because it is not in contrast to this that Alternative Economics exists.) The two sorts of economics in question, then, are Classical Economics and post-Classical, or Keynesian Economics. (Let us put neo-Keynesian Economics aside for the time being: it might be followed, before we know it, by, some new sect—Eclectic Economics, perhaps.) Between them, these make up the body of theory that for the greater part of this century has ruled economic policy.

Or perhaps it would be more accurate to speak of what has passed for 'economic policy'. For arguably it was only the Great Depression of 1931 that brought anything resembling economic policy into being. And that this should have been so was but a reflection of the character of Classical Economics: for this is characteristically subjective in its orientation, being concerned with the economic behaviour of individual people. Economic man is its masthead symbol, and Marginal Utility Theory (the notion of price determined at the margins of people's wants) governing the laws of supply and demand was its apotheosis. The ideal of equilibrium was necessarily central to Classical Economics (it was assumed to be a natural tendency in the sum of things), and Adam Smith's Hidden Hand of the market was the *Deus ex machina* whereby Providence ensured the benignity of the price mechanism.

It was the bafflement of classical economists by the horrendous unemployment of the Great Depression—many and ingenious were their speculations about the causal relations involved therein—that cleared the way for Keynesian Economics. The difference could be expressed by a concern, not with unemployment, nor with how the Hidden Hand had mysteriously failed, but rather with employment. Economics became objective—and, some would say, heartless. The economy was a reality, out there: it could be aggregated into statistical entities like Gross Domestic Product and growth rates of National Income.

Keynes knew, better than his subsequent critics, that the psychology of individuals could lead to rampant inflation, given the new mechanics needed to ensure full employment in an objectified economy. (Perhaps even 'stagflation' would not have surprised him.) But to have explored such a relationship would have led him into the deepest of waters. It would, indeed, have led, through an insight into the questionable integrity of our culture, to doubts about the validity of either Classical or post-Classical Economics. And, in retrospect, the whole episode seems so sad, for what else was it but a playing out, in yet another dimension, of the perennial and insoluble dualism of our culture: of subjective and objective, of person and world?

In any case, it would be naïve to expect much clarification from some hypothetical resolution of the two components of the dichotomy of economics. It is in the nature of such thinking to reify its ideas—to make a thing out of 'the Market', or out of 'the Economy'—and, once reified, that thing is separate from its conceptual opposite and has its own life and obeys its own laws.

Hence the inner workings of the Keynesian Economy remain unknown, and probably unknowable, territory. We would be unwise to specify even that they hinge on greed. The politically near-disastrous argument between Mrs Thatcher (and her closest advisers) and her Chancellor, Mr Lawson—as to whether the economy (or, actually, people) would respond best to a rising exchange rate and a falling rate of interest, or to a constant exchange rate and a rising rate of interest—may serve to illustrate the point. The truth is that nobody knows. It's not in the book. All that is known, more or less, is that either course could (fingers crossed!) be disastrous because the whole 'thing' doesn't actually hold together.

So, a main consequence of the objectification of economics has been that it has let mathematics into the act, lending a spurious truth to an academic discipline. This is to say nothing against mathematics: it is no doubt the greatest game in the repertoire of *Homo Ludens*. Rather, it is only to confirm Kant's premise, that we manufacture the forms by which we live.

Unfortunately, however, it has served to foster the illusion amongst economists that they are the physicists of social science.

Value could thus be treated as the social property of objects—and economists, as observers of the social science, were value-free. This, in its turn, would have been harmless enough had it not meant that the makers of economic policy became bewitched by figures. Indeed, the capacity of figures to bewitch us—as, say, they bewitch the Stock Exchange— would have to be part of any economic theory with any serious claims on our attention.

However, I would not advocate the pursuit of any such theory. There is a deeper reason arguing against its possibility. Economics may fancy that it is concerned with the allocation of resources through the measurement of value; but how we measure things is itself a measure of our values. For this reason, values are a feature of our environment, of our social climate, rather than the social property of objects. Unlike love (perhaps), value alters when it alteration finds. It is indeed Time's fool.

The American monthly trade figures, published well after the event (and subsequently amended) will affect the value of the dollar. Such valuation tells us as much about the valuer as about what is valued. It is essentially tautologous. Thus, any change in the value of the dollar is affected by second-guessing on the part of those who deal in currencies. By some reports, as much as 90% of deals on the foreign exchanges are presently in such speculative money. Measurement (of anything) attracts its own *aficionados*—and 'the Economy' just such *aficionados* as it deserves. It is not everybody's language, and those who do not speak it will hold other values.

Now, for all I know, all this may be commonplace to the advocates of Alternative Economics. I'm certainly not entering into any critique of their corpus of ideas, here or elsewhere. But it may be protested that the grandfather of the movement, Fritz Schumacher, whose famous essay on Buddhist Economics in *Small Is Beautiful* was arguably the inspiration of it all, was surely not ignorant of economics. He was, after all, for a time Keynes' distinguished collaborator. 'Buddhist Economics' was written from a sound knowledge of economics generally, and what it did was to ridicule one of the cornerstones of that discipline.

That is to say, it implicitly called into question the notion of labour as a 'factor of production'—a component of the system that conventionally gained its reward at the margin. Schumacher showed that for some cultures, work was its own reward; it could thus lack the teleological property that gives economic value its validity. One might say that Schumacher de-reified the economy by its *reductio ad absurdum*. Having done so, however, he did not go on to offer an alternative theory. In Wittgenstein's terms, he was content to show the fly the way out of the fly-bottle.

And so I think it should be. The first need is to show the nonsense of that no-thing, the Economy. It may be asked, what do we then put in the place of economics to explain how everything connects? Well, why should we assume it must all connect, when all the evidence suggests it doesn't in any holistic sense? After all, when we have each divided ourselves, why should we expect Providence in the form of economics to come to our rescue?

All that an abandonment of economics as a false science would do would be to focus attention on the everyday particulars of material life: on banks, firms, actual markets, wages, profits, resources, taxes, etc. The consequence might well lead to a questioning of many institutions, virtually devoid of meaning, which have necessitated the fabrication of economics to make some sense of our way of life. But that would be a different story.

So we arrive at my reason for wishing that the protagonists of Alternative Economics showed more knowledge of the original. I am just afraid they might be heading down a dead end. For I question whether there is any economics for Alternative Economics to be an alternative to.

Chapter Five

About Some Books

The Tragic Century

WE LIVE IN more than usually desperate times and we sense a *fin de siècle*, but with a vengeance. A century of the Somme, the Holocaust, Hiroshima, of Communism and therewith the collapse of 2,000 years and more of idealism, down to the almost casual massacres of Rwanda: such a century would have torn the guts out of any civilization. But our foreboding is of still worse than this: the Earth itself cannot imaginably sustain us and our ways of living. Even so, not many people, perhaps, would characterize our condition as tragic. Yet it is so. And, paradoxically, because it is so, we have grounds for encouragement.

I am thinking of tragedy as the Greeks understood it—or, at least, as we infer they understood it, from the only dramas that have come down to us from one time and place, but a most significant time and place: the Athens of a hundred years before Plato.

It is of this that Bernard Williams writes in *Shame and Necessity*. He does so not as a historian, nor even as a philosopher (of which he is one of the most eminent alive), but simply as someone willing to share his erudition with others. This has the incalculable advantage of allowing us to speculate how his insights might conform with others', as indeed they do; for Williams makes it clear that any perusal of the ancient Greeks is to be justified by what it might teach us about our own condition. And he concludes: "In important ways we are, in our ethical situation, more like human beings in antiquity than any Western people have been in the meantime." For, like them, "we know that the world was not made for us, or we for the world."

Bernard Williams quotes with approval his own mentor, Hermann Frankel: "In the Iliad man is completely part of his world." The antithesis of Self and not-self, Frankel said, did not yet exist in Homer. Yet by Plato's time, it did; and, into the bargain, in Plato's tripartite structure of the Self, Reason held the commanding position—dominant in its masculine quality over femininity, closer as this was to nature and feeling.

Somehow, it was out of the 'shame culture' of Homer's time that this separation of the Self emerged. Shame, Williams explains, is the peculiarity of Self: "In the experience of shame one's whole being seems diminished", and he illustrates it with the simple case of bodily nakedness. Alongside shame there is guilt. Shame concerns one's personal standing; guilt one's social standing. But in Greek antiquity one word covered both concepts.

Then, over a period of 500 years, this dualism developed, to be codified by Plato and so incorporated as the keystone of Western civilization. Homer himself began the decline from our essentially transient experience of the world by fixing in writing the meanings of words—and in particular the graven distinction between verbs and nouns: hence between doing and being. "I fear we'll not get rid of God before we get rid of grammar", said Nietzsche.

This would at least be a thesis congenial to what Don Cupitt develops in *The Time Being*. At all events, by the time of Sophicles and Euripedes the conditions for tragedy, as Bernard Williams describes them, must have been in place: the condition in which human and divine are in opposition. Such a condition arises from the exigencies, the necessities, generated by dualism: the compulsions of the social on the personal, of the outer on the inner.

"The Greeks", Nietzsche said, "were superficial out of profundity." (He also contended, famously, that Christianity had robbed us of the harvest of the ancient world.) They, the Greeks, knew they could not know everything, and so the gods implicitly served an aetiological purpose. But with dualism the gods lost their place, and there began the process of accountability by man for his own position in the world, a process that is only coming to an end in our own day and age. In place of Greek supernaturalism, we now have the principle of uncertainty; in quantum mechanics we have the breakdown of the detached relationship of observer and observed, whilst chaos theory and much else are returning us, as Williams says, to a neo-Homeric mentality. And if on the moral plane all this should seem regressive, he points out that for the Greeks, slavery (say) was not even a moral question; it was simply one of those manifold necessities implicit in the maintenance of any way of life: a necessity, he might also have pointed out, comparably accepted in Western societies today of an emerging underclass and of permanently high unemployment.

IT IS EQUALLY with our illusions of the Self that Don Cupitt's book is centrally concerned. He speaks in this light, not only of the death of man in the last forty years, but even of "the death of metaphysical theology as we have known it . . . God's second death". *The Time Being* is an extraordinary book because, coming from so close to the Anglican Establishment (Emmanuel College, Cambridge), it is if anything a barely disguised encomium of Buddhism. It is to the Buddhist philosophy of self, then, particularly as we have it from Dogen and Nagarjuna, that Cupitt looks to rescue Christianity from the malaise about our private being into which it has all too logically fallen.

And yet, Cupitt observes, this malaise has coincided with the triumph in late capitalism of what stems directly from the theology of Augustine and Liebnitz: a harmonization of person and world, originally reserved for Heaven, but now seemingly attainable on Earth. Cupitt gives the astounding impression that all that is remiss with this triumph is the abandonment of religion itself. He would remedy this by grafting on to Christianity what repeatedly he calls "post-Buddhism of the sign"—a phrase he never explains, but which, I take it, must refer to Wittgenstein's philosophy, in which, in any case, Cupitt's texts and precepts are steeped.

The book is extraordinary also in the honesty with which it follows through its premises. "Our whole culture," he says, "has been founded on a falsehood"—the falsehood of dualism. Again, "We need—don't we know it by now—a religion without God, that is a religion without absolutes, without perfection, without closure, without eternity." He insists, as of course does Buddhism, that all is transience, nothing but transience, and on the contingency of all our actions. He refers us (as also does Bernard Williams) to Peter Brown's excellent *The Body and Society* for an understanding of how early Christianity helped mould the divorce between body and soul and shifted the centre of gravity of human frailty from death to sexuality.

Cupitt says, "Mind is a cultural fiction" (which surely it is, as also a function of the Self). He affirms that language is "outsideless" (which, after all, is how Wittgenstein concluded the *Tractatus*), just as it is social, not private, and that we cannot use it to predicate anything metaphysical. As for time, it is, he says, nothing more nor less than the time of our being; and religion is nothing but a therapy, a cure, for our bewitchment by language. In brief—although I think he is misinformed in his one major reservation concerning Buddhism and language—you might say that we have here as good a crash course in Buddhism as many a textbook devoted to the subject.

What it has to do with Christianity, I'm not so sure. One understands that Don Cupitt is central to a growing movement of Anglican Christians that would dispense with God. They may have a point in the perspective of history, but Cupitt does not argue this here. (This book is only one of a trinity.) Instead, he proposes "radical Christian humanism", but he scarcely discusses what he means by it. In truth, it is hard to know in the end what his position is on the central notion of the Self—and I hope I have not done him any injustice in the foregoing. Intellectually, he rejects any substantiality in the Self, but (in his own terms) he is so acculturated to it that he seems reluctant to lose it altogether, and it reappears as the individual.

You, the reader, should pay him the compliment of trying to find this out for yourself, for the book is almost indigestibly rich. Only beware that, in a footnote, he jokes about his own reputed inconsistencies, and perhaps this is the price to be paid for his trying to bring philosophy and theology together again after some two millennia of separation.

Where I think Cupitt unquestionably falls short is in his social understanding. Not that he overtly addresses this, beyond some superficial remarks about cities and alienation; but, contrary to all he urges about how we make our own world within the limits of language, he takes our social structures as given by the language of nineteenth-century liberalism. This leads him to what can only seem (today of all times) a ludicrous eulogy of the politician as a species: he who of all people is most alert to the transience of things. It is one thing (rightly) to assert the importance of politics; it is something else ineluctably to bring Harold Wilson to mind as a model to humankind. Suffice to say, the practice of politics requires an arena appropriate to its limitations.

What is truly disturbing, however, is that 'radical Christian humanism' seems quite unaware of today's environmental concerns. Cupitt never mentions these, and perhaps so long as one retains, for all one's radicalism, Christianity's soteriological thrust (its concern for individual salvation), environment will never be much other than a question of stewardship.

By much the same token, moreover, it seems to me that ultimately Cupitt is unaware of the tragic nature of our condition. (To be fair, nor does he believe in its perfectability.) "Tragedy is cultural", he says, as if we can invent or disinvent it. But that it is cultural is itself tragic, it seems to me. Our very outsidelessness, against which we indeed cannot fight, is truly tragic. That we are the masters of our own fate, doesn't seem to amount to much! Again, given the social nature of language, as Cupitt remarks, "by a striking paradox I can only fully get hold of my own ideas by getting rid of them." We are perforce strangers to ourselves and must always search for the ground of our being.

By contrast, Victor Seidler, in *Unreasonable Men*, is fully aware of the contemporary significance of ecology: he knows it undermines the Cartesian tradition, the whole apparatus of modernism. He also provides a sound application of Wittgenstein's thought. "His work remains the most significant challenge to a Cartesian tradition," Seidler says. (Perhaps contrary to the impression that Cupitt leaves, for Wittgenstein the Beginning was not the Word, but the Deed.) Seidler clearly sees that ever since Bacon spoke of torturing Nature on the rack until she yielded up her secrets to an avowedly masculine philosophy, the Cartesian Self has been "the central figure of modernity" and all its mechanistic works. His book is about the crisis of identity in this Self in the face of feminism.

Seidler, then, sees feminism as a challenge to much more than male political domination. He sees it, rather, as a refutation of the primacy of Reason in the Platonic model of that Self which has set the terms of Western culture. It is the very premises of social theory that are at issue, and the atomization of the individual associated with current epistemology. Wittgenstein's contribution to this process is fundamental: "In reminding us of the complexities of our everyday experience, Wittgenstein is returning us to the aspects of experience that we too often discount and devalue. It is as if in the Cartesian tradition we are continually losing our ground so that we have continually to find ways of grounding ourselves in experience. Put differently, Wittgenstein returns us to a humanity that we have learned to forsake too often in the wake of modernity."

This is as much as to say that our feelings must be admitted to social theory—and where, one wonders, might that leave economics? Probably just about where Schumacher left 'Buddhist Economics'! Seidler does not attempt to tell us this. His book, rather, is impregnated with a reassessment of Marxism, and maybe this will yet be part of a new synthesis of thought. Indeed, his is a seam of many riches. As Seidler says, for instance, if only we could learn not to say "boys don't cry", the world might yet be turned upside-down. But you should be warned that there is an academic textbook flavour to his writing. That it is to be recommended despite this, is some indication of its worth.

SO WHAT DO a philosopher, a theologian and a sociologist have in common? Perhaps primarily, that they are not really writing philosophy, theology or sociology—and it is a small miracle that their books have been published at all in an age when reductionism is rampant in publishing. (One wonders if Nietzsche, that non-philosopher, would be published today?) It is hard for a reader to be nourished on non-dualistic, on holistic, thought, outside the Buddhist aegis. It just seems to me that these books, taken together, are evidence that the ground is shifting under our feet—and such a shift is for the good. If we can be brought to realize the fundamentally tragic nature of the illusions we harbour about our tenancy of the Earth, we might learn to take a delight in it again.

On Being and Becoming

IRIS MURDOCH'S book *Metaphysics as a Guide to Morals* is about the difference between 'is' and 'ought', about analytic and moral philosophy, and hence about the spiritual vacuum in which we find ourselves. It is a theme which could be made to cover the history of Western philosophy—and, indeed, theology. It is through the eyes of a spectrum of philosophers that Iris Murdoch chooses to treat the notion of morals. Hers, however, is not an historical approach as such, but rather a way of shedding light on her question by testing it against salient thinkers of the last 200 years, from Hume (as foil to Kant) to Derrida, yet always by casting back to, and projecting forwards from, Plato. Within these approximate bounds, the book is a veritable *tour de force.*

Iris Murdoch looks at this separation, of fact from value, from the starting point of the lost wholeness of our consciousness. She discovers the vestigial evidence of this unity in art and in religion. Such wholeness is intuited, although the evidence for it is always of a limited whole, because our perception of it cannot transcend the act of perception itself. We cannot know reality itself, which always lies behind appearances, and Plato's seminal parable of the Cave, whose dwellers can see only the shadows cast on its walls by the sun behind them, is the recurrent motif of the book.

The author is fully aware that her premises sound old-fashioned, with all their talk of 'virtue', but this, taken with the absolute fairness of her presentation—indeed, her generosity to all points of view—provides the gentle shock she seeks to administer in order that philosophy might be brought to take morality seriously again. Metaphysics, she stubbornly contends, is to be justified as this process of pointing beyond— and this despite her acute awareness of bad metaphysical art and false religion.

It follows that morality prescribes the individual. It is in the individual that our moral sense inheres. (Public morality is, albeit problematically, merely a matter of axioms.) Awareness of the Good, Plato's supreme form of virtue and reality itself, is a property of the soul. The trouble is, however, as Iris Murdoch herself almost casually notes: "For purposes of ethics, and indeed in general, we lack a suitable philosophic view of 'consciousness' and 'the self'." She herself throughout draws no distinction between the individual as, at best, a limited whole playing a contingent part in some scheme of things, and the singularly Christian notion of the person autonomously imbued with an immortal soul. The whole of Western philosophy could arguably be seen as a stubbing of toes against this obstacle.

Indeed, this ignorance in Western philosophy (for which the dualism of Self and World is pivotal) of Eastern thought, is increasingly extraordinary. In this respect, Iris Murdoch's book is perhaps a tell-tale of how the wind is changing. She makes frequent, if general, references to Buddhism (in particular to Zen); and for her, as for Buddhism, suffering is the crux of the matter. She also has the warmest of spots for Schopenhauer, the only Western philosopher of substance to take any note of the Eastern tradition. As Murdoch notes, however, nobody followed Schopenhauer in this respect. (Subliminally, Wittgenstein might have done so, since Schopenhauer was one of the very few philosophers in whom he had any interest and, as a growing body of study demonstrates, the affinities between Wittgenstein and Buddhism are astonishingly close.) Perhaps the West awaits its new Tyndale to render Nagarjuna into vernacular English.

At all events, insofar as Iris Murdoch discloses her own position it is to speak of herself as a 'Buddhist Christian', and even to entertain the notion of a Christianity without God. (Perhaps, in this connection, the ordination of women priests will open the path to a non-dualistic Christianity?) Certainly, the process of Christian demythologization is under way.

The journey on which Iris Murdoch takes us through the philosophy of our era, in her attempt to restore a respect for ethics through metaphysics, is an immensely enriching one. On this journey she illuminates Descartes, Kant, Hegel, Schopenhauer, Freud, Marx, Husserl, Heidegger, Kirkegaard, Nietzsche (to whom alone I think she is less than just), Sartre, Derrida, Simone Weil, Martin Buber and many more; whilst, in the course of it, she gives us the benefit of a fascinating essay on King Lear, as well as a disquisition on Anselm's Proof of the existence of God. I myself am particularly grateful— and not a little enhumbled—to have been given an insight into Adorno and his "fearless passivity".

I think she is least satisfactory in her treatment of Wittgenstein, and this is perhaps because he gives her thesis most trouble. Whereas she can say of A. J. Ayer, by whose brilliance she admits to having been dazzled as a student forty years ago, that his work now seems to her "dotty"—one could say of him, as has been said of the Vienna Circle, that he has "nothing to be silent about". Wittgenstein's silence "whereof one cannot speak", on the other hand, seems, in all its implications (not least for the practice of meditation, but also for the scale and complexity of our social structures) to leave her baffled. She has the greatest of respect for him, but half admits that she is not competent to discuss him.

In fact, I'm sure she is, but I don't think she wants to face the challenge of his dictum (which she doesn't even cite) that the purpose of philosophy is to rescue our intelligence from its bewitchment by language. This is, of course, the nub of the case against metaphysics and, far from belittling the realm of value, it confirms it. ("It is clear that ethics cannot be put into words. Ethics is transcendental." That is to say, it has to be lived.) But it also suggests the possibility that much of which metaphysics treats, including all our ideals, is built on sand—as might be expected of a civilization enjoined to render unto Caesar what is Caesar's and to God what is God's. Only consider the case of economics and all the harm this pseudo-science has done this last half-century, based on a simplistic utilitarian idea of the value of 'happiness'!

Iris Murdoch is none the less clear that this is the end of the Cartesian era (Wittgenstein has ensured it), and maybe the end of the Aristotelian era also. But she also ventures that we are closer than for many centuries to Plato. I trust she means by this, to a realization of the indissolubility of fact and value—though, in that case, a reference to the more organic thought of the presocratics might have been more apposite—and to a coming together again, at long last, of philosophy and theology (or at least of faith). But I also trust that she does not have in mind the progenitor of idealism, from which this century has been the ultimate sufferer, for in that case I for one would find myself with Don Cupitt (whom she quotes generously enough): "So far as all the varied movements of the day have a theme it is anti-Platonism. Plato impressed upon the entire history of Western thought . . . a supernaturalism of meanings (essentialism) and of knowledge—all of which has suddenly come to seem utterly absurd and unendurable." In fact, if it's the case, as was said by Whitehead, that the whole of Western philosophy is nothing but footnotes to Plato, so much for the West!

Frankly, I do not find it credible, as Iris Murdoch would have me believe, that every second of my life is lived morally, concerning virtues somehow derived from the absolute value, the Ideal Form of the Good. This, however, will not prevent me from recommending this book from the bottom of my heart. It is at once extraordinarily rich in reflection of our times and as harbinger of a new springtime.

A Heroic Voice

IVAN ILLICH is one of the few hard men of the new age of thought and it is therefore all the more quizzical that his stance in his book, *In the Mirror of the Past*, is from the perspective of twelfth-century Europe. I do not suggest he is hard-hearted, but he is intellectually uncompromising; he has no time for the pseudo-substantial, or for shibboleths—even New Age ones. He is concerned with that without which our everyday discourse could not occur: with everyday reality. But from his historical perspective, in the mirror of the past, he shows that much we take for real nowadays has not always had this authority. The book is an indirect assault on the successive and continuing metaphysics of our culture and all its fictitious 'stuff'.

Being a collection of talks (about a score of them) given over the past twenty years to various professional groups, it would be hard to say the book has a theme. If it has a thread,

I would say this consists of the inexorable atomization of Western society, of its loss of the 'commons'; and the tracing of this process is through language and the way it has been used. The greatest of all the metamorphoses thus revealed is that from the oral to the literate age. It is to the alphabet we owe our present-day cult of the individual.

Perhaps of special interest is the light Illich sheds on how the clerks, particularly those of the rival monasteries of Cluny and Gorz, prepared the way for Gutenberg—and hence for our possessive and industrialized society. Language preceded experience. The clerks in Charlemagne's time—and only then—began the process of separating word from word in the manuscript, and then sentences, paragraphs, chapters and so on (even indices: there is, alas, none in this book), until by the time of Gutenberg the text already stood apart from the reader, and knower from known. A famous landmark on the way, after all, had been St Augustine's astonished discovery that he could read silently, and so in private. The key Western notion of the substantial Self and all its accompanying metaphysic was ready to be born.

Ivan Illich, then, has been talking by invitation to various professional groups—educationalists, health practitioners, economists ("The alternative to economics cannot be reduced to alternative economics"), architects, information technologists, bishops—all people who have most stood to benefit from the literate notion of reality: from its notion of Man as a composite of needs ("we need needs"), including, latterly, of 'development'. We are not told what his hearers' reactions were, but one can only surmise they must largely have been one of incomprehension. For, of course, he set the cat amongst numerous pigeons—and left them to get on with it. By challenging, as he does, the very categories, the spheres of life, of these activities, he threatens to leave them meaningless.

Illich does not excuse himself from his own implacable gaze. He recants somewhat on *Deschooling Society*, explaining he would not argue for the elimination of schools, but rather for their disconnection from the social establishment. It is, however, when he comes to the latest metamorphosis, in which he fears we now find ourselves, that he shows himself as human as the rest of us. This is the metamorphosis from the literate to the cybernetic age—and he doesn't like it, and wants little or no part of it. For it signals the end of all conversation, and is tantamount to the extinguishment of our feelings. ("I am concerned about how to keep awake in the computer age.") He sees it, moreover, as coincident with the extinction of the profound and specifically Christian notion of 'a person'; and, in the most eloquent pages in the book, enjoins his audience (Lutherans) to give no further approbation to such fetishes as 'human life on Earth', to which this managerial mentality has perverted that notion. Readers should be warned, in fact, that Illich includes many of the most strongly held views of the Alternative Movement in his critique of systems analysis.

Yet one wonders if this despondency is not a consequence as much of the weakness as the strength of the point in history at which Illich chooses to take his stand. He passionately professes himself a child of the literate age and its Christian humanism; but was not the ultimate split between spirit and matter, which is what the cybernetic age portends, implicit in the literate age and the kind of knowledge it perforce pursued? It was, surely, the alphabet and its power of storing the human voice that marked the beginning of the process—though the twelfth century might indeed have seen the beginning of its flowering. When schools in Plato's days turned from *musike* to the written page, the die was cast and the commons was lost. What became subsidiary at that point was meaning, for meaning (as Illich says) is forever on the wing, is never fixed; it inheres in the speaker—and in the bard. "The meaning of a word", as a certain philosopher of our time has said, "is in its use in the language." No dictionary can encage it. And it is the loss of meaning, not knowledge, that is at the root of our present malaise.

Whether or not there is force in these comments, however,

they but touch the surface of this book. The erudition is bewildering (a bibliography would have been helpful to ordinary mortals: though there is a useful summary of Illich's own works). It is not an easy read, nor a sustained polemic; but it is to be mined, and mined again.

Spirit and Causation

> The spirit, said St John, is like the wind that bloweth where it listeth, and you hear the sound of it, but whence it cometh and whither it goeth, you know not.

IT IS OFTEN said that ours is a godless society, but this clearly is not entirely so. We now have proof, not maybe of the existence of God—almost that, though not quite just yet—but of how very much people would like to understand him.

The evidence lies in the long stay at the top of the Best Sellers list of *A Brief History of Time* by Stephen Hawking, a book of popular science that ends with the sentence, "If we find the answer to that, it would be the ultimate triumph of human reason—for then we would know the mind of God." It's true that the author, Lucasian Professor of Mathematics at Cambridge, has subsequently confessed that he wanted to delete that last phrase, though his publishers persuaded him otherwise. Publishers, after all, know their business; it has been reckoned that that last little phrase alone has sold at least half the copies of this generally very lucid book. So there's no doubt God had a hand in it.

The 'that' in the above-quoted sentence refers to a unified theory of the forces governing the universe. Such a theory, it appears, would be able to explain in one equation both computers and nuclear power, and would therefore be very useful; and (depending upon God) might even lead to still greater benefits.

It is at this point in his exposition, and at the very last, that Stephen Hawking falls back upon those whose business he says is with 'the why': the philosophers. He complains that their knowledge has failed to keep pace with the scientists', whose business is with 'the how'. This tardiness of philosophers in explaining why scientists are doing their thing has resulted in even the greatest philosopher of the twentieth century (as Hawking rightly calls Ludwig Wittgenstein) resigning himself to the statement that, "The sole remaining task for philosophy is the analysis of language." What a comedown, says Hawking, from the great tradition of Kant and Aristotle.

The sole task! It just happens to embrace the how and the why of our thought. In this respect Wittgenstein was, to coin a phrase, a quantum leap from Kant: or, to put it another way (indeed, the analogue of it), as great a paradigm shift as quantum theory was from relativity. It was a leap from dualism to non-dualism. Between the form of ideas (which allowed 'numinous' to enter through the metaphysical back door of Kant's philosophy) and the scalpel of language, there lies an abyss of difference. "When the answer cannot be put into words, neither can the question be put into words . . . It is not how things are in the world that is mystical, but that it is," etc. But that is just for the record—except to add that Wittgenstein would have viewed the distinction between the 'why' and the 'how' as pernicious.

Yet, whilst on the topic of language, it is intriguing that Hawking should not have noted Niels Bohr's remark during his controversy with Einstein (when Einstein could not accept quantum theory, because "God does not play dice with the universe"), namely: "There is no quantum world. There is only an abstract quantum-mechanical description. It is wrong to think that the task of physics is to find out how nature is. Physics concerns what we can say about nature."

Wittgenstein himself was apparently unaware of the contemporaneous development of quantum theory (amazingly so, for his own background was in engineering and mathematics): but such is the compartmentalization of academia! However, as early as the *Tractatus* (1919) he had pre-empted any scientific claims to knowledge of 'the mind of God'. (Perhaps he was also historically closer in time than Hawking to Lord Kelvin's classic gaffe, pronounced shortly before the discovery of Relativity, that our knowledge of the physical universe was now effectively complete.) "We feel", Wittgenstein wrote, "that even when all possible scientific questions have been answered, the problems of life remain completely untouched. Of course there are then no questions left, and this itself is the answer."

In fact, the curious thing about scientific knowledge is why its holders should have come to think it has such an extraordinary significance—and why we laymen troop so dutifully behind them. Part of the answer may be sought in the story of Newton's miserable life. In fact, the only inadequate part of Stephen Hawking's book is the three cameos he gives, as an addendum, on the lives of Einstein, Galileo and Newton; and that on Newton is not merely inadequate, it is a disgraceful travesty. "Isaac Newton was not a pleasant man," he begins, and continues in that vein. No hint is given that Newton was a tortured individual, starting with the wretchedness of his abandonment in childhood and continuing, in the prime of his life, with his desperate (and nearly fatal) alchemical experiments to try to recover the sense of any meaning that he realized was being lost in his work—to say nothing of his fearful suppression of his heretical form of the Christian faith (Arianism, which disavows the Trinity). One cannot but wonder what Newton was running away from: nor, too, generically, what scientists with their ever more remote abstractions are escaping from.

A clue to this mentality may be found in Galileo's then radical contention that, "the book of nature is written in geometrical characters." Once Descartes, the primogenitor of rational idealism, had devised the algebra to furnish this crusade, there was no stopping it. For the weakness of humankind—indeed its congenital sickness—is metaphysics (the use of language to express what language cannot say), and mathematics in the Galilean sense is archetypically metaphysical. That it is internally so seductively logical is to say nothing about its depicting the world, except that mathematics is obviously one of many useful tools for that purpose. Such use, however, remains a stipulation, a prerequisite, not itself an observation of the world. It is a stipulation, moreover, rooted in dualism: in the user of this tool being separate from that upon which it is used, in Cartesian dualism of mind and matter.

Mathematics as metaphysics likewise requires the invention of Nature—just as economists with more obviously laughable (or more sinister) consequences had to invent the Market. What is 'out there' is a presumption of classical science, as also is the notion of mind. This, in turn, implies the idea of Creation and of the Creator—i.e., God: He of the 'mind' that so bewitches the reading public.

Hawking, in fact, makes much (unassuming) mention of God: it is only surprising not to find Him in the index. And yet the author really does seem quite muddled. He comes at the last, and with due caution, to the view (derived from the quantum theory of gravity) that God's role in creation must at the least be problematical: that "the universe would be completely self-contained and not affected by anything outside itself. It would neither be created nor destroyed. It would just BE." (his capitals) Or again: "But if the universe is really self-contained, having no boundary or edge, it would have neither beginning nor end: it would simply be. What place then for a creator?" Yet, as that last all-too-tempting phrase in his book reveals, Hawking simply cannot bring himself to discard all recourse to God. No wonder he was in two minds whether to delete the phrase.

One wonders whether Professor Hawking realizes that Eastern philosophy came clearly to his so cautious conclusion some two and a half millennia ago, and that it was codified by Nagarjuna in our second century AD (as "Form is Emptiness, and Emptiness is Form")? Nor is a concept of the Creation deemed meaningful in that philosophy. Or perhaps Wittgenstein might also be allowed his laggardly say, anticipating Professor Hawking's questions by a bare seventy years (again from the *Tractatus*):

> The sense of the world must lie outside the world. In the world everything is as it is, and everything happens as it does happen . . . For all that happens and is the case is accidental . . .

> If we take eternity to mean not infinite temporal duration but timelessness, then eternal life belongs to those who live in the present . . .

> How things are in the world is a matter of complete indifference for what is higher. God does not reveal himself in the world . . .

And much more besides, all driving towards the non-separation of mind and body.

NOW, MY POINT in all this is actually not to offer a review of Stephen Hawking's book. As far as a layman can judge, it is excellent of its kind and, until those last few unsure pages, shot through with humour and even compassion. The point, rather, has to do with the spiritual; and in particular with the relationship between the spiritual and causation. For Professor Hawking's book, by dealing so honestly with the notion of the Creation that has been central to our Western mindset, encourages renewed inquiry into how the mystery of our existence must concern our everyday lives.

Science, indeed, having been fixated upon the given of 'Nature', could be deemed an involuntary denial of concern for the spiritual; for the Creator is thereby reduced to a cause, even if *primus inter pares*, in Nature: the Determinator (the source of Newton's unease). Yet even in Christianity, which accepts the Creation, the greatest of its servants, its mystics, have known that in any train of causation they must look behind the veil. Between causation and spirituality, indeed, there is a primal connection.

Obviously, if causation implies a Creator, then all derives therefrom—but seemingly, Hawking says, it doesn't. Conversely, should the agency of causation itself be insubstantiable, we are left with a puzzle. And indeed, in Western philosophy, since Hume's demonstration of the insubstantiability of causation (some 1,600 years after Nagarjuna)—"We are entirely determined by custom," Hume concluded, "when we conceive an effect to follow from its usual cause"—this has become a commonplace of Western philosophic thought. Hawking implicitly accepts it. For Hume, this led to a profound scepticism, as in all honesty it must (belief, after all, is the prerequisite of certainty)—always provided, that is, we assume it is 'things' that are thus changed by indefinable causes. But if 'things' are no more than reifications—that is, mental constructs without substance—a quite different understanding dawns. If, for instance, a thing is a thing only by reason of its not being another thing (as Nagarjuna showed) we are left with the interdependence of all 'things'. Which is to say that we are left with nothing but relationships—not relationships between things, but of transient realities. And in this ever-changing scene nothing changes of itself, nor is any one thing the cause of another's change: yet causation is constantly at work. That, I suggest, is where the spiritual is to be found. And we look for it but vainly in the mind of God.

If this seems obscure, I suggest its recognition is to be discovered in the notion of environment which—against the tide of now-discredited reductionism—is struggling to the surface of contemporary life. That is, the notion of a set of interdependent and mutually sustaining relationships, with no measurable values attachable to any of its discrete parts. It follows that an environment is not to be appropriated and that, in so far as it is, its spiritual character will be lost. Yet, it should also be noted that an environment as a whole cannot be diminished by an appropriation of its parts—as, say, by an access of scientific knowledge of the universe—because any such instrumental action will but generate the conditions of manifold further interdependent relationships. The world, to paraphrase Wittgenstein, must wax and wane as a whole. And so the environment is not lightly to be abused. Knowledge may lead only to darkness.

One last word, and one that returns us to Stephen Hawking. He suffers from a terminal disease, hard for anyone without direct acquaintance with it to imagine. On this account his book has been received with much public sympathy. I myself, my wife having succumbed to this illness, have reason only to be frank with my criticisms; but by the same token I can all the more warmly commend his book, not just to any amateur of science like myself, but because, by its innate courage, it takes science to within sight of being out of currency. This leads me to suggest that when a unified theory of the physical forces in the universe is contrived, as I suppose it might be, the message we get from it could be: please, leave the universe alone. Let it just BE!

Then, regardless of 'the mind of God', we could together get on with cultivating our spiritual garden. Which also resonates with Wittgenstein: "The real discovery is the one that makes me capable of stopping doing philosophy . . . the one that gives philosophy peace."

Chapter Six

Resolution

A Western Falun Gong?

IT WAS ALL so simple until the Wall fell. We had our differences, of course, but they were contained within the mechanisms of the Cold War—even our differences over atomic power: no one thought you could disinvent the bomb. But now, slowly, we are losing our way, as it might dawn on someone on a small boat at large on the ocean that their compass is faulty. The goal of 'Europe', in particular, seems not so much undesirable, as implausible, with the diplomats negotiating the last Peace. The natural reaction in these circumstances is just to make sure the mechanics of living still work: the taxes are imposed and spent, the schools educate, money is counted, houses are built, science is researched, the trains run, the old are kept alive and the young tolerated (if not understood), the clocks keep time, the jails are filled: all is flat, stale and profitable. Above all, nothing should change its meaning. It is, in other words, the perfect soil for the lowest common denominator of a tabloid culture.

So it might indefinitely continue—except that words do, and will, change their meanings. Amazingly, for instance, the education policy the British Government has been pursuing, of literate tests at the earliest age and of simplistic school inspections as unnerving as they are false, has never stopped to consider what the role of schools in education actually is. But there is a whole suppressed debate here waiting to be held—a debate questioning what education is. And, too, should houses be built where they have always been built? And if so, can the idea of a city remain unchanged? Will work, when it has largely moved from the factory floor, or the office, mean what it does now: just a factor of production? When God is finally dead, will not science also came to mean something else?—for why should it bother with a game of dice?

Meanwhile, in this stagnation, we are patently at an historical cusp: between the history from 1789 to 1989 and of the history to come. Of course, this historical division, like all the others—Renaissance, Enlightenment, Middle Ages, etc.—is a contrivance that does small justice to historical continuity and primarily serves the purposes of the *zeitgeist*. (And we love taxonomy: it helps us to count.) But the announcement of an epoch in advance has, at least, the merit of an open declaration that things must and will change, and significantly so.

The inexorable change then, readable in the cards, is one of scale: of the withering of the dinosaurs. And the strength of this perception lies in the question of our epistemology: in the failure of what we take to be knowledge to make sense of the world, even to provide for our survival in it. For it is what we assume to be knowledge that has generated all our specialisms, which derive from the manifold reductions of parts from their wholes, so separated as to be measured and studied and reproduced by all and sundry. In brief, our knowledge is dualistic: it privileges the measurable—such that we want what we produce, rather than produce what we want—and such knowledge incubates alienation. It is ensnared in the equivocal and ephemeral relationships of words and the world. And in practice, above all, it magnifies our ignorance of what we do not reify. 'Environment', which cannot be reified, announces, with all its forebodings, the coming breakdown of the knowledge that has structured our society and its culture.

Ironically, if predictably, this reductionism of our knowledge entails a magnification in the scale of our functions in the world. Once the parts of any whole are separated from that whole's constraints, they can be multiplied to serve their special function, so long as that function has its separate uses. And not the least of those uses, generally speaking, will be power. Since the uses of power are highly unpredictable, the knowledge whereby it has been obtained cannot but be suspect, at best. And at worst the metaphysics of knowledge can lead to the madness of a Great War.

Yet the pedigree of reductionistic knowledge was set out for us by Descartes in his 'Method' as a prelude to his establishment of the subject—the Self that thinks—in this dualistic system of knowledge. Our present moment, indeed, is the high tide of the Self—hopefully its swan-song also. Disillusion, not only with the madness of war, but with ideology—the continuation of war by other means, to invert Clausewitz—whether Fascism, Communism, Socialism, or even Liberalism, has left the field to solipsism. "There is no such thing as Society," Margaret Thatcher could say (alas for Karl Marx; it was to counter just such a then fashionable outlook, 200 years before, that he began his labours on *Das Kapital*. Thus does the whirligig of time bring in its revenges—or it does so, anyway, in our dualistic culture).

So now the Self wanders where it will in its desert. Indeed, this was all Wittgenstein could find at the end of the logic of his youthful *Tractatus*: the Self as a dimensionless point. "The world is my world." Out of such self-induced despair he concluded (or almost concluded) ". . . anyone who understands my propositions eventually understands them as nonsensical, when he has used them, as steps, to climb up beyond them. (He must, so to speak, throw away the ladder after he has climbed up them.)" Anyone who knows the Buddhist parable of abandoning the raft when one has reached the other shore will find the similarities uncanny.

Wittgenstein's actual conclusion, rather, was "Whereof one cannot speak one must be silent," and, as he made clear elsewhere, it was his silence alone that was pregnant of meaning.

Nowadays, and for the time being, the Self searches for itself, appropriately enough, in the always ephemeral world of fashion: in being conformably unconformist. And not just in clothes or other accoutrements: more dangerously, in ideas. Ideas like the Third Way, or Communitarianism, or psycho-everything. And it finds itself in 'spin', in the appearance of reality: reality itself has no reality. The word is in eclipse.

Compatibly with this Self there is still a lingering sense of guilt at being without any ideology, any overarching idea, to guide one's actions. There are unconvinced resorts to the old formulae (warm beer as the shadows lengthen on the cricket field, etc.), and equally unconvinced reproaches to those who may attempt them. As much could be said of and for the old religions. And yet the Green-tinged change that is inexorably occurring in our epistemology, the sense that the old knowledge is failing us, that ultimately science doesn't have the answers, indeed that it might be the problem, is inducing a tangibly growing sense of spiritual need in ever more people. Can the Earth itself survive our use of it? Or rather, can we ourselves survive that use? And who are we, anyway, that we should survive? All in all, we are experiencing a change in the meaning of what it is to know something.

NOW IF ONE must hazard a reason why the old religions— or at any rate, those of the Peoples of the Book—do not speak to us in our spiritual need, brought upon us as it is by the failure of our old notion of knowledge, it is that they stem from the same stock. Causation, the very idea of it, is what religion and science hold in common—and ultimately a First Cause, which even contemporary scientists speak of as the Mind of God, or a Law of Everything. What does not stem from this root—such as the Orphic religion of old, or the 'Hindu' faiths—is rooted in power and in societies, such as the caste system, dependent thereon: and their gods are necessarily tricksters. I doubt they could hold much comfort for us nowadays. Yet there is a 'faith' that transcends all these handicaps—that is neutral so far as causation is concerned, and that eschews proselytization—and is of growing appeal to the beleaguered West. I refer to Buddhism.

I refer to Buddhism, but I do not proselytize for it—if for no other reason than it would be futile to do so. For Buddhism is virtually asocial. It flourishes, or simply survives, in many very different cultures. Obversely, in Lhasa there are mosques which provide for the Muslims who butcher the staple diet of the local Tibetans—a phenomenon of mutual tolerance almost incomprehensible to the Western mindset.

Buddhism likewise is manifested in manifold cults—over 600, I believe, at the latest count. Yet what these cults, all with their different rituals and practices, might be said to hold in common is an underlying sense of reality—in which meditation, in one form or another, constitutes an important element.

So, if Buddhism has nothing to say about Society—and it hardly does: indeed, there would be difficulty even in finding a word for it—what purpose could there be in summoning it to the aid of our hapless Western world? Well, we are perhaps already more Buddhist than we realize. We no longer put any trust in ideology. And has there not been much talk of 'the end of History'?—which might be better understood as the end of our accepted way of understanding things. And have we not learnt from quantum mechanics that if we pursue the composition of substance we but terminate in a void, and that subject and object lose their meaning?—and does this not conform to Buddhist teachings about reality, about the contingency of all things, that no thing has its own being and everything is interdependent, subsuming the insubstantiality of the Self. Combine all this, then, with the dwindling credibility of the Nation State and all its works, the growing (but frustrated) importance of the local. For example there is a serious proposition that the state of California should be split into two—in which case the southern part would be Christian and the northern part Buddhist. And where California leads . . . But in case anyone should get the wrong idea about all this, some lines of Nagarjuna*, generally accepted as the greatest interpreter of Buddhism, might be borne in mind:

> Buddha never taught anyone
> Anything.

and

> Believers in Nirvana
> Are incurable.

So it would be worse than rash to think of a Buddhist political movement, even (as might be supposed) under a Green disguise. Nevertheless it is not fanciful to envisage a Buddhist, or a neo-Buddhist, society emerging in part of the West, comparable to many such diverse societies in the East. Whether such societies were or were not known as 'Buddhist' would be secondary.

Yet from these promising beginnings, little more might emerge without some intentional encouragement. The facilitation that Buddhism can offer for the transformation of our society, then, is one that stems from the sense of reality on which it rests. This sense of reality is not dualistic, but holistic. As such it must treat of matters that are small of scale, for only thereby can some other 'method' than Descartes' reductionism contain the always manifold realities of any situation. Holistic knowledge is only accessible on the small scale. And, as it happens, there are many non-ideological movements in the world today urging that action in our daily lives should be on a smaller, more local scale—and these movements are not, conventionally speaking, revolutionary.

For instance, the urgently needed decentralization of power in Britain today is stalled largely by a paralysis of thought about how the massive transfers of money and power from the centre to local authorities at all levels should take place. This

---

* Nagarjuna: *Verses from the Center*, trans. Stephen Batchelor

issue has been shelved since the Roskill Report on Local Income Tax of the mid-seventies was confined to oblivion. But the need remains, overshadowing the whole ineptitude of Parliament and its diminution by 'presidential' government, and the transfer in question is not revolutionary: or if it is, Switzerland is the most revolutionary country in Europe.

Again, the practice of education on a human scale is not revolutionary, though it would overturn the deluded and faux-progressive Comprehensive movement of post-war Britain; and Denmark has a system we could copy in every smallest detail, not excluding the cycle paths integral to every school, or rejection of the examinations that blight the British child; and I do not think Denmark is a revolutionary power.

Hypothecated revenue is not revolutionary, though Whitehall dreads it as a threat to its authority—but this too is changing. The return of the value of development land to the community that has generated it is not revolutionary, or if it is, John Silkin, who in 1975 incorporated it into the Community Land Act, was the most unlikely of revolutionaries—and I take leave to doubt if Margaret Thatcher, who annulled it as her first legislative act, understood it beyond her hatred of planning itself.

The support of small-scale farming—indeed the gardening as much as the farming of Britain—would hardly be revolutionary, though abandonment of the cult of high technology (including the cannibalization of livestock) might seem extreme to the Ministry of Agriculture, implicitly immersed as it is in its culture of the large-scale. The re-connection of industry to its locality, lost by the thoughtless abandonment of the old Rating System, would not be revolutionary. And so on.

In other words, the field of action is overflowing. And the way Buddhists of the future can change the world (as it must be changed) is not by learning about 'Buddhism'—which might almost remain optional—but by changing the meanings of words. And the words whose meanings they have to change are such as 'education', 'democracy', 'community', 'farming', 'cities', 'countryside', 'wealth', 'knowledge', 'faith', 'environment', 'belief', 'peace', 'enlightenment', 'work', and scores of others. And last, but foremost, the first person singular—the 'I' word, never to be used without some context.

How might this be done, this constructive deconstruction of our false knowledge? Perhaps, just by the use of the internet for thoughts, for pensées. Or also by the writing of *koans*. Even perhaps some Haikuesque poems. It is all a matter of soaking the atmosphere in direct and local responses to the everyday events of life. Something like the Falun Gong that has the Chinese Communist Party so worried. Above all, there is no need for political parties and their organizations. Their detritus can be left to history. Better to trust to our Buddha nature!

On no account should this be taken to mean the establishment of some new cult. As for the actual Falun Gong, I have no idea what belief, if any, it holds—beyond its being spoken of as somehow 'Buddhist'. As such, I would not expect it to prescribe the kind of society in which people should live. At most, I would expect it, by its questioning, to moderate the authoritarian Confucian Communism of today's China. But I think we are as deeply frozen in our dualistic mode of thought as are the Chinese in theirs, and as much in need of a questioning of the meanings of our language.

If, as I think is the case, Bernard Williams is right that in our ethical situation we are "more like human beings in antiquity than any Western people have been in the meantime", then we are back at the great bifurcation of East and West. If it is any consolation, the pre-Socratic gods of that time—all twelve of them on Olympus and the one with horns, Pan, outside it—did, *pace* Einstein, play dice with the universe. So I am certainly not recommending a revival of that religion: but only that we should quietly conspire to change the meanings of that whereof we should be silent.

Appendix

A Short Bibliography

of works directly influential on this book

St Augustine	*Confessions*
Stephen Batchelor	*Buddhism without Beliefs*
	Verses from the Center (Nagarjuna)
Peter Brown	*The Body and Society*
Fritjof Capra	*The Web of Life*
T. J. Clark	*Farewell to an Idea* (Modernism)
William Cobbett	*Cottage Economy*
Don Cupitt	*The Time Being*
René Descartes	*Discourse on the Method*
H. L. Finch	*Wittgenstein*
Edward Gibbon	*Decline and Fall of the Roman Empire*
D. Goleman	
& R. Thurman	*Mind Science: an East-West Dialogue*
Chris Gudmunsen	*Wittgenstein and Buddhism*
D. Harvey	*The Condition of Post-modernity*
Stephen Hawking	*A Brief History of Time*
Ebenezer Howard	*Garden Cities of Tomorrow*
Ivan Illich	*In the Mirror of the Past*
Allan Janik	
& Stephen Toulmin	*Wittgenstein's Vienna*
David Kalupahana	*Nagarjuna: The Philosophy of the Middle Way*
Leopold Kohr	*The Breakdown of Nations*
Ray Monk	*Ludwig Wittgenstein*
Iris Murdoch	*Metaphysics as a Guide to Morals*
Friedrich Nietzsche	*The Birth of Tragedy*
	Twilight of the Idols
Fernando Pessoa	*The Book of Disquiet*
Theodore Roszak	*Ecopsychology*
J. J. Rousseau	*Emile*
E. F. Schumacher	*Small is Beautiful*
	A Guide for the Perplexed
Victor Seidler	*Unreasonable Men*
Charles Taylor	*Sources of the Self*
F. Varela	*The Embodied Mind*
Bernard Williams	*Shame and Necessity*
Peter Winch	*The Idea of a Social Science*
Ludwig Wittgenstein	*Philosophical Investigations*
	Tractatus Logico-Philosophicus

Also by Maurice Ash:

New Renaissance

The first Renaissance was a powerful conjunction of Humanism with the forms of classical antiquity. It led, perhaps inevitably, to the Enlightenment, entailing the separation of Man from Nature, with all its resultant fragmentation and loss of cohesion characteristic of our times.

The possibility of a new Renaissance arises from the urge for wholeness to which this fragmentation has brought us, in conjunction with the rediscovery of a philosophical tradition at least as sophisticated as our own, but different at root.

This new conjunction of West and East offers an escape from the impasse in which nowadays we find ourselves. The West of itself cannot escape from the flybottle of its own making.

Green Books 206pp ISBN 1 870098 00 5 £6.95 pb

Journey into the Eye of a Needle

In *Journey into the Eye of a Needle,* Maurice Ash encapsulates a lifetime of learning into a series of essays on the spiritual and ecological crisis facing humankind. He believes that all contemporary issues are interrelated: the destruction of the environment can be traced to the way we use language; and the overweening power of the state results from our failure to sustain community. He argues that the current spiritual vacuum in the West stems from the loss of meaning in people's lives, which in turn is intimately connected with the very nature of dualistic thought in which we are trapped. The emergence of meaning lies in a profound rethinking of the way in which we conceive of ourselves, and our relationship to the world.

Green Books 96pp ISBN 1 870098 35 8 £7.95 hb

Also by Maurice Ash:

The Fabric of the World
Towards a Philosophy of Environment

Everyone is talking about the environment. But what do we mean by it? This is the subject of this perceptive and provocative book.

Maurice Ash shows us how the nature of our thinking has led us to conceive of 'the environment' as something separate from ourselves, upon which we can act; and yet, he says, it is just this kind of thinking that has brought about the despoliation of the earth.

The author argues that the environmental crisis is engrained in the language of our political, social and economic structures. In his search for the hidden agenda of the Green movement, he shows the need for us to include the reality of the spirit. Only by doing so, and by re-establishing the importance of local life, may be hope to maintain the fabric of the world, and cease exploiting it for our own ends.

Green Books 112pp ISBN 1 870098 42 0 £8.95 hb